RED OR GREEN
New Mexico Cuisine

RED OR GREEN
New Mexico Cuisine

Clyde Casey

Clear Light Publishing
Santa Fe, New Mexico

To My Wife Millie
For over 50 years my loving companion,
Without whom my life would have little meaning

Copyright 2007 Clyde Casey / Clear Light Publishing
Clear Light Publishing
823 Don Diego
Santa Fe, New Mexico 87505
www.clearlightbooks.com

First Edition
10 9 8 7 6 5 4 3

Library of Congress Cataloging-in-Publication Data

Casey, Clyde.
  Red or green : New Mexico cuisine / by Clyde Casey.
     p. cm.
  Includes index.
  ISBN-13: 978-1-57416-090-1
  ISBN-10: 1-57416-090-7
  1. Cookery, American--Southwestern style. 2. Cookery--New Mexico. I. Title.

TX715.2.S69C386 2007
641.59789--dc22

                          2007001762

Front cover design: Marcia Keegan and Carol O'Shea
Interior design & typography: Carol O'Shea

TABLE OF CONTENTS

 **INTRODUCTION**

"Red or Green?" This is the most commonly asked question in New Mexican restaurants. It means, do you prefer a red or green sauce on what you ordered. Generally red chile sauce tends to have a fuller, richer flavor and is milder. The green chile sauce has a sharper, clearer bite. Make no mistake about it—your choice can make a significant difference in the flavor of your dish. The relative hotness of red vs. green is by no means universal, however; a newcomer to this wonderful food should ask the waiter/waitress which sauce is hotter, since this can vary from restaurant to restaurant and even from day to day.

Since the 1960s, when I first traveled to New Mexico, I have been in love with its exciting cuisine. From the early 1500s, when the Spaniards first arrived, this distinctive fare has been in a constant state of evolution. The result is a unique blend of many culinary arts that combine Native American, Spanish, French, Ranch Chuck Wagon, Mexican and Mediterranean influences. Today this rich savory cuisine is known world wide, and each year millions of visitors to this "Land of Enchantment" learn to appreciate it for the first time when they hear, "Red or green?"

According to the New Mexico Genealogical Society, when the pilgrims came ashore at Plymouth Rock, the first Thanksgiving had already taken place in what is now New Mexico, 23 years before, in April of 1598. Historian Sheldon Hall says that a party of 400 men plus perhaps 200 women, under the leadership of Juan de Oñate, trekked across the barren expanses of what was then Northern Mexico. On the last four days they had no water, and visions of exhaustion and death assailed them. These colonists finally came upon the Rio Grande Del Norte. There, according to Gaspar Perez de Villagara, "They threw themselves into the water and drank as though the entire river did not carry enough water to quench their terrible thirst." Within a few days, they came in contact with the local Manso Indians and exchanged gifts and food. They thanked their deity and the generous Indians by holding a festive dinner, a Mass,

and a ceremony appropriating all the lands drained by the Rio Grande for the King of Spain.

New Mexico is a land of mixed cultures. The most dominant historically are the Native American, Mexican and Spanish. New Mexican cuisine today still reflects its roots in Native American cuisine—a basic combination of chile, corn, beans, squash, wild fruits, nuts and game. The arrival of the Spanish brought chickens, pigs, cattle, olives, grapes, rice, sugar, wheat, ground cinnamon and a variety of other spices. As the years progressed the French and other newcomers added diversity to what is today a rich and spicy yet delicate and distinctive style of cuisine.

I hope that those who share my love of this festive food will find these recipes worth trying. In my first two cookbooks, I presented Southwestern flavors of the past and present. In this book, I continue to present both traditional and modern dishes that will acquaint you with New Mexico's unique cuisine. I have also included some basic recipes that can be modified in an infinite variety of ways; Southwestern cooking can be an extremely creative as well as flavorful endeavor. You will also find delicious ways to prepare fish and wild game as well as holiday recipes. With these recipes, you can experience the excitement of preparing bold-flavored foods and sharing them with friends and family. There is no substitute for home-cooked food.

New Mexican cuisine can be very healthy. Because the ingredients are simple, it is possible to retain the unique complexity, color and texture of each while creatively producing delicious dishes. I encourage lean cooking methods: broiling, steaming, grilling and baking. I also recommend the use of vegetable cooking spray and the selection of monounsaturated cooking oils, such as canola (rapeseed) oil and olive oil. Although I have added salt to most of the recipes, I like to use it sparingly and allow herbs and spices take a greater role in the flavoring and aroma. When you prepare New Mexican food at home, you can control the fat and carbohydrate content, unlike when you eat out and are unaware of the restaurant's cooking procedures (you can bet they are the quickest and easiest methods). If you are a lover of the vibrant flavors, colors, tastes and textures of this cuisine, you will find that you do not have to worry—you can have your tortillas and eat them too.

Chile

Chile forms the heart and soul of New Mexico cuisine. These peppers are vegetables of the pod-bearing *Capsicum* species. The term "chile" is applied to the smaller, hotter varieties of *Capsicum*; the milder larger varieties include bell peppers, which have no heat. Chile peppers have been a part of the human diet in the Americas for centuries, having been domesticated several thousand years ago as one of the first cultivated crops. The fiery hot flavor of the chile is most intense in its seeds and inner membranes or veins; removing these cools the heat somewhat and is recommended in preparing chiles for cooking.

Nutritionally, chile peppers, particularly the red, are very rich in the antioxidant vitamins A and C. Red chile is also a source of beta carotene. Low in calories and high in potassium, chile may speed up your metabolism and help you burn more calories. Chile can make you feel good in other ways as well. The capsaicin in chile stimulates the brain to produce endorphins, which produce a sense of well-being. Capsaicin can also be used as a topical analgesic to reduce pain from arthritis and other conditions. It is thought by some that chile may aid in treating asthma and allergies and in helping to prevent heart disease and cancer. Also, new data shows that chile by itself does not necessarily bother the stomach.

Do not confuse ground or powdered chile (chile with an "e") with chili powder (chili with an "i"), which generally consists of ground chile with cumin, salt, garlic powder and other herbs or spices added. The word "chili" also refers to dishes containing chile as well as other ingredients such as beans and meats.

What do you do if you take a bite that is too hot? Milk, yogurt, sour cream, ice cream or starches such as bread or rice will help. Alcohol also dissolves the hot capsaicin that causes the burn, but, of course, use that with care.

Fresh chile is seasonally available in the late summer and early fall, but canned, dried and frozen chile is available year-round. New strains of chile

are developed frequently; there are hundreds of varieties, and each has its own distinctive taste. Some New Mexico recipes blend several different varieties to produce a taste not available with only one type of chile. In general, New Mexicans want the flavor of the chile, not just the heat.

Preparing Chiles for Cooking

Whenever possible work with fresh chiles. In selecting chiles, look for brightly colored, blemish-free pods. You must prepare them properly for them to be at their best. Chile peppers have an outer skin that must be removed before cooking. They are only easy to peel if they have been roasted so that the outer skin is blistered and charred, which causes it to separate from the flesh. Because it takes as long to do a dozen or so as to do one, you should do a batch at a time. A barbecue grill is preferable, but you can also use your kitchen broiler.

Make a slit in each chile to allow the steam to escape and arrange them on the grill or a baking sheet (a layer of foil on the pan makes easier cleanup) and set the heat to broil. Turn the chiles as needed so they are blistered all over. It is fine if the skin becomes black. Try not to disturb the flesh underneath the skin while turning. When they are ready, place them into a heavy plastic bag (allowing a minute or so of cooling first so the plastic doesn't melt!). Let them sit in the bag at least 20 minutes while their internal steam loosens the skins. The more delicate types, such as poblanos, should be dipped in cold water immediately upon removal from the heat to stop the cooking action, then peeled immediately. A side benefit of this process is the wonderful aroma that will emanate from your kitchen.

After roasting, you do not need to skin the chiles or remove the seeds before storing them. They will keep fresh for several days in the refrigerator, or you can freeze them with their skins on, preferably in single-recipe-sized amounts. When you are ready to use them, allow them to thaw or run them under hot water and the skins practically slide off.

After removing the skins, if you plan to use the chiles whole, as in **Chiles Rellenos** (See p. 118.), slit each whole chile carefully and gently remove the inner white veins and seeds but leave the stem. For other purposes remove the stem.

A word of caution when preparing chiles: the capsaicin oil (primarily located in the seeds and inner veins) can burn the flesh, so use rubber or disposable kitchen gloves. You may also need to protect your eyes from the vapors.

In the late summer, if you live in the Southwest, particularly New Mexico, you are likely to be able to buy green chiles directly from a local vendor, who will roast them for you on the spot. This is the easiest way of all to put up chile; just take it home, cool it, separate it into freezer bags and freeze it (keeping some in the refrigerator for immediate use, of course). You can also purchase frozen green and red chile in some groceries and on-line. Frozen chile can be sent Federal Express priority overnight. See "Where To Buy Chiles" in the **Appendix** on pages 245–46.

Varieties of Chile Peppers

Chile peppers differ in flavor and heat intensity depending upon type. The mildest is the Anaheim (New Mexico No. 6) and the most fiery is the habanero. Some variance of hotness exists within each type, but each generally falls within a certain range of fire. For example, one jalapeño may be hotter than another, but no jalapeño will be hotter than a habanero. Color is not necessarily an indicator of hotness. The following list is based loosely on the Scoville heat units of capsaicinoid content of individual varieties of chiles. The numbers indicate a rank from very hot at 10 to mild at 1. These rankings are approximate, as individual batches of specific varieties of chile will show some variation in hotness.

Chile Pepper Heat Scale
    HOT
10. habanero, Scotch Bonnet
9. Santaca
8. Tabasco, Cayenne, Thai, Chile de Arbol
7. serrano, Amarillo, Tabasco® Sauce, crushed red pepper, habanero hot sauce
6. jalapeño, chipotle
    MEDIUM
5. Sandia, poblano, yellow-wax, cascabel
4. ancho, Española, pasilla
3. NuMex Big Jim
2. Rio Grande
    MILD
1. New Mexico No. 6, formerly known as Anaheim

Some of the chiles listed in the heat scale are not typically used in New Mexico cooking but were included because they are fairly commonly used in other parts of the country and in other types of cuisine, such as Japanese and Thai. Here are some varieties you will find in New Mexican cooking:

Anaheim chiles

A type of New Mexico chile (see New Mexico chiles). The mildest variety of chile, these are now known as New Mexico No. 6 (sometimes just New Mexico).

Ancho chiles

Anchos are ripened, dried poblano chiles. These are the most popular dried chiles in Mexico. They vary from sweet to moderate heat.

Big Jim chiles

A type of New Mexico chile (see New Mexico chiles).

Cascabel chiles

Fresh cascabel chiles are hard to find in the United States. They are round, about 1½ inches in diameter. Sometimes dried Anaheim chiles are labeled "cascabel," but that label is incorrect and can cause problems, because the cascabels are much hotter and have a distinctive flavor all their own. When dried, the cascabel chiles have a nutty flavor.

Cayenne chiles

These small, narrow red peppers (about 3 to 7 inches long and pencil-thin) are usually ground into "red pepper" or "cayenne pepper." Cayenne is very hot and typically used as a seasoning, particularly in Cajun cooking.

Chipotle chiles

Chipotle chiles are smoked and dried jalapeños with a very wrinkly brown appearance. Because of their unique smoky taste, they should not

be substituted for if a recipe calls for them. They are often canned with tomato sauce and called *en adobo*. Don't let the smoky flavor fool you, these chiles are hot!

Habanero chiles

Originally from Havana, habanero chiles are said to be the hottest peppers in the world. Similar to the Scotch Bonnets, these lantern-shaped chiles have a fruity flavor, if you can taste anything through their heat. Not for amateur use.

Jalapeño chiles

Taking their name from Jalapa, the capital of Veracruz, Mexico, these popular chiles have a good amount of heat—ranging from hot to very hot—and rich flavor. Dark green and similar in appearance to serranos, these chiles are about three inches long and mostly feature rounded tips. The sharper the tip the hotter the chile. Rarely the chief components in a sauce, they are used for flavor in variety of Southwestern dishes. Green jalapeños appear in late summer and ripen into red chiles in the fall. The red ones have a much richer, warmer flavor that the green. Jalapeños are sold fresh, pickled and canned, but try to find fresh ones; canned jalapeños aren't as fiery or as tasty. When smoked and dried they are called chipotle chiles (See chipotle chiles).

New Mexico chiles

Many varieties of chile are grown in the state, including jalapeño, cayenne, ancho, pasilla, mirasol and del arbol. There are, however, a few varieties that bear the name New Mexico chiles. These are relatively slim and range from five to eight inches long. They vary in color from light green to deep green to bright red, depending upon maturity. Because they are sometimes twisted in appearance and their flesh is thin and fragile, they are not normally stuffed. They have a tough skin, which peels off easily after roasting. Like the jalapeños, these green chiles turn red when they mature, when they are sometimes referred to as *chiles colorados*. They are then available in dry form, either powdered or whole, often in dark red wreaths or ropes called *ristras*. There are two main varieties of New Mexico chiles, New Mexico 6 (formerly Anaheim) and Big Jim.

New Mexico 6 (formerly Anaheim) chiles

The mildest variety of chile, these taste pretty much like bell peppers with a bit of a bite. They add flavor to cooking but very little heat. These chiles were named

Anaheim after the town in which they were canned at the turn of the century. Canned "mild green chiles" are typically this variety.

Big Jim chiles

When green, Big Jim chiles are available in mild, medium hot and hot varieties. At harvest time, these chiles are the ones most commonly available fresh (and freshly roasted) in New Mexico and the Southwest. Be sure to ask about the heat when you buy—their names describe their heat. Hot Big Jims carry almost as much heat as jalapeños.

New Mexican-type cultivars include NuMex R Nak, NuMex Big Jim, Sandia, NuMex Conquistador, NuMex Sweet, NuMex 6-4, and NuMex Joe Parker. Each has its own heat level and taste.

Pasilla chiles

Pasilla means "little raisin" in Spanish. These thin, red-brown chiles are about 6 inches long and are used instead of poblano chiles in some recipes. When dried, pasilla chiles are black in color and called *chile negro*. They have a dusty, raisin-like taste and are of medium heat.

Poblano chiles

Poblano chiles are heart-shaped, more like a bell pepper, and a little darker colored than the New Mexico Big Jims. These tasty chiles are somewhat sweeter and hotter than all but the hottest New Mexico green chiles and their skin isn't as tough. With their deflated bell pepper shape, Poblano chiles are especially good when used for stuffing and are the chiles most frequently used for chiles rellenos.

Red pepper flakes

Red pepper flakes, or crushed red peppers, are just what their name suggests, flaked dried red chiles. Most chile flake mixtures are quite hot, so use with care. Normally used as a seasoning, red pepper flakes can add a bite and bring out the flavors in almost any type of cuisine.

Serrano chiles

Hotter than jalapeños, these little chiles have thin skins, so you don't have to char, steam or peel them before using. They range from middling green to brilliant red when ripe. Extremely hot, these chiles are usually shorter and thinner than jalapeños and are a mainstay in salsas.

Canned vs. Fresh

Most of the recipes in this book call for New Mexico green chile. One 4-ounce can of green chile is the equivalent of 4 or 5 fresh or frozen New Mexico green chiles or 3 fresh or frozen Big Jim chiles. The sizes of fresh chiles will vary, so use your judgment and adjust the amount to taste.

Corn

For centuries American Indians have held corn in highest esteem for its food value as well as its religious and symbolic significance. Corn meal is used to accompany prayers and even as a prayer itself in many tribal ceremonies. Scientists believe corn was originally developed by people living in Mexico many centuries ago. It was started from a wild grass called *teosinte*, which looked very different from modern corn. By collecting and cultivating those plants best suited for human consumption, these early Native peoples gradually developed the corn that looks familiar to us today. From Mexico, corn (or maize as the Indians call it) gradually spread into the American Southwest and down into South America. Corn traveled with Columbus and other explorers back to Europe, Africa and Asia.

The diet of the native peoples of the Western Hemisphere was built upon the "Inseparable Three Sisters"—corn, squash and beans. This provided them with an excellent nutritional balance, especially with the addition of nuts, fish and game. We can enjoy this trio today; try the **Indian Corn Casserole** on page 101.

Corn can be roasted, boiled, grilled and steamed. Hominy, a dried corn processed with lime, is a central ingredient in many traditional dishes. Cornmeal, made from the nutritional part of the kernel, the endosperm, is used in breads and, of course, tortillas.

In New Mexico, corn comes in approximately two dozen varieties with colors ranging from white to blue to yellow to bright red. Each color has a different significance to the Indians and is used for different purposes. Sweet yellow corn is eaten on the cob. White and pale yellow are used for flour, hominy, tortillas, tamales and bread. Blue is used for

baking, drinks, **Hopi Piki Bread** (See recipe p. 70.) and blue corn tortillas. Red is sometimes used for traditional posole. Some groceries now carry tortilla chips in all of these colors, and you will notice that each color has a slightly different taste.

To make tortillas, the Indians soaked corn in water containing enough lime to make the skins come off (See p. 65 for a modern recipe for **Corn Tortillas**). These softened kernels were then ground into a smooth dough called *masa* and patted into very thin flat round cakes. Masa is also patted into cornhusks to make the outside covering for **Tamales** (See recipe p. 107).

Beans

Consider the bean a low-fat, protein-dense, easy to prepare staple of New Mexico cooking. Inexpensive, high in fiber and complex carbohydrates with no cholesterol, beans make sense for everyday eating. There are many varieties available in a wide variety of colors, often in mottled patterns that are dotted or speckled. They are round, oval or flat, long and thin, or plump and kidney-shaped. Their flavors range from the robust to hearty to earthy. Some are even delicate and subtle. New Mexican cooks are cooking with an ever-broader selection of beans and pairing them with some unexpected partners. Our growers are experimenting with foreign and lesser-known varieties, finding that they enrich our nitrogen-poor soil. Try my **Four Beans & a Pea Cassoulet** (See p. 97.) for a special treat that is a great example of the use of these often underrated and overlooked legumes.

Beans were first domesticated about 7,000 years ago in Peru and southern Mexico. As these peoples traded with each other and with peoples to the north and south, bean cultivation spread all over North and South America, then traveled with the explorers to Europe, Africa and Asia. The cultivation of beans required some nomadic tribes to settle in villages in order to tend the crops. During the times when game was scarce, beans became their critical source of protein. Combined with the simple carbohydrates in corn, the complex carbohydrates in beans created an ideal body fuel, made complete—with the addition of squash seeds, piñon nuts, chiles, wild berries and wild plants—even when meat was unavailable. The following types of beans are often used in Southwestern and New Mexican recipes:

Anasazi beans

One of the most popular of the modern boutique beans, the Anasazi bean is also called the Aztec bean, Cave bean, New Mexico Appaloosa and sometimes Jacob's Cattle. This attractive purple-red and white bean cooks in about ⅔ the time of an ordinary pinto bean to a creamy even pink color. It has a sweet mild full flavor and a mealy texture, perfect for any New Mexico recipe.

black beans (*frijoles negros*, turtle beans)

These small dark beans have a hearty flavor. They are often used in South American cooking, and their very dark purple-blue color makes them attractive in salsas.

black-eyed peas (cowpeas)

These are the seeds of the cowpea, an annual vine. Their tan coloring with black spots gives them the name "black-eyed." According to legend, black-eyed peas are supposed to provide good luck when consumed on New Year's Day.

garbanzo beans (chickpeas)

These rounded, beige-colored beans have a nutty flavor and a buttery texture. They are often used in salads and are also a noted ingredient in many types of Middle Eastern and Indian cuisine such as hummus and falafel.

pinto beans (*frijoles*)

These attractive brown-speckled beans have a pale or pinkish background when dry. Cooking changes them to a dull pink or grey-brown. A staple of Southwestern cooking, pinto beans are what you will usually find on your plate in restaurants, whether by the side of enchiladas or wrapped in a burrito.

In general these beans are interchangeable in the recipes that follow. I have selected certain ones for certain recipes because I prefer their taste, color and consistency in those particular recipes, but this is a matter of personal preference.

There are several different ways to cook dried beans. These are described in "Preparing Dried Beans" on pages 113–14. Choose the one that works best for you.

Going Wild in the Kitchen

Just as they did in the early days of this western land, hunting and fishing still provide an important portion of the menu of many New Mexicans. Although the wild buffalo no longer roam free, we have bear, elk, deer, and antelope to fill our freezers. Big game hunters come from all over the world for a chance to bag a trophy elk or deer from our bountiful meadows and pastures. For game birds, New Mexicans hunt ducks, geese, wild turkey, pheasant, quail, dove and grouse. Fishermen head to the lakes, rivers and mountain streams for bass, bluegill, carp, catfish, perch, Kokanee salmon and trout. Some still hunt small game, including rabbit, raccoon, squirrel and porcupine.

For a New Mexican sportsman, nothing compares to the thrill of the chase. Golden aspen and the scent of the forest floor in autumn, the sight and sound of a flock of geese overhead or the distant bugle of an elk— these are what make the hunt special. The hunt becomes an indelible and mystical adventure. On those very special occasions when the game bag is bulging and the creel full with the harvest of the forest, field, lake or stream, the hunter's family shares the excitement of the chase through the provided bounty, just as the families of Native American hunters did long before the Spaniards came to this enchanting land. Even in this day of scientifically designed foods, there is no fare to match the savory store from nature's pantry.

Fish and game, properly cared for and properly prepared, provide a variety of exciting dishes. See pages 145–66 for ideas and recipes.

From Grape to Glass
New Mexico Winemaking

Very few people are aware that New Mexico was making fine wines long before the planting of California's vineyards. More than three centuries ago, as early as 1602, New Mexico vineyards produced wine from Mission grapes. The 1880 census recorded 3,150 acres of vineyards under cultivation in New Mexico, with an annual production of 905,000 barrels of wine per year. At that time, New Mexico ranked fifth among America's wine-producing states and territories.

Bernalillo, located 18 miles north of Albuquerque, was the center of New Mexico's wine production throughout the eighteenth and nineteenth centuries, with up to 6,000 grape wine plantings reported in the 1870s. In his book *El Gringo*, published in 1875, W. H. Davis describes Bernalillo's clarets as better than French imports. The Christian Brothers monastic order operated a winery in Bernalillo until the 1950s and produced much of New Mexico's sacramental wine. The Italian Rinaldi and Gros wineries, late in the eighteenth century, and the French Mallet family winery, early in the twentieth century, also contributed to winemaking history in Bernalillo. The Mallet winery is still standing on the southern side of the Abenecio Salazar Historic District.

Wine producing slowed when the disastrous flood of 1897 was followed by a severe drought, and farmers began raising other crops. By 1914 the Rio Grande Valley showed wine acreage to be a mere 8 acres, and Prohibition provided the final blow. Gradually in recent years wine production has become profitable again, and in 1990 New Mexico produced 700,000 gallons of wine. Today the state has more than 5,000 acres of wine grapes. When today's acreage of vines mature, production will approach 4,000,000 gallons per year.

In the 1970s and '80s, changes occurred in and around southern New Mexico in the Mesilla Valley. French, Italian, German and Swiss winemakers invested in New Mexico. Encouraged by the surge in popularity of wine, they planted new vineyards all over the state.

New Mexico's climate is well suited for the growing of wine grapes. The arid desert climate, with an average rainfall of less than 9 inches per year, combined with an extensive Rio Grande River irrigation network, allows viticulturists to control the amounts of water needed to produce excellent grapes. Vineyards flourish in different types of soils and at various elevations. Our soils range from deep clay loams over a rocky

volcanic base in southern New Mexico to shallow sandy loam in the northern part of the state. Elevations vary in the viticultural areas of the state from 3,700 feet to 6,400 feet.

New Mexico has other advantages for grape-growing that most desert regions do not. The sun is very intense because of altitude and cloudless skies. Also, the state experiences a large variance between daytime and nighttime temperatures; altitude causes nighttime temperatures to drop 30–35ºF below daytime temperatures. Other arid grape-growing regions do not experience such contrasts. Because of the long cool nights, vinifera and hybrids maintain a high acid to high sugar balance. New Mexico's yields per acre are high, averaging 6 to 8 tons in a given season. A long growing season, intense sunlight, abundant irrigation, and most of all, the cool nights of the desert—all contribute to the making of good wines.

While the Mission grape predominated in the early years of New Mexico winemaking, it has gone by the wayside for the most part, and only a few plantings continue here. Now, several varieties, including both Vinifera (in southern New Mexico's warmer climate) and the hardier French/American hybrids (in the colder northern part of the state and higher altitudes), are thriving.

New Mexico Wines

Today local vineyards produce gold-medal wines. Here are the wines currently produced in our glorious climate. These are the types of vines and wines that are making New Mexico one of the premier wine grape-growing areas of the nation.

Baco Noir

Northern vineyards and wineries specialize in growing and making wines from the French hybrids. This outstanding hybrid red grape with distinguished character produces wine with a flavor as powerful as a Cabernet Sauvignon. Baco Noir goes well with hearty flavors such as rich barbecued ribs.

Cabernet Sauvignon

New Mexico's varied climatic conditions have proved to be excellent for growing this, the noblest of all grape varieties. Cabernet Sauvignon, along with Chardonnay, produces one of the world's most desirable wines. With its flavor primarily being black currant with classic cassis and cedar characteristics, this dark red wine, known for its high levels of extract and tannin, is often blended with complementary varieties such as Merlot. Cabernet Sauvignon complements red meats, hearty red pastas, strong-flavored cheeses and dark chocolate.

Chardonnay

Rich is the word that best describes Chardonnay and explains its popularity. Its aroma is distinct yet delicate and difficult to characterize yet easy to recognize. Depending on where the grapes are grown and how they are fermented, the flavor of Chardonnay can range from semi-sweet to sour and from heady to light, with hints of apple, tangerine, lemon, lime, melon and oak. Grown in the cooler winemaking regions of New Mexico, the Chardonnay grape is also an important component in champagne. There are some 100% Chardonnay champagnes, labeled *blanc de blancs*. Chardonnay is also used by sparkling wine producers who want a champagne-like wine. It goes well with poultry dishes, light red meat dishes and rich creamy sauces.

Chenin Blanc

The Mesilla Valley and Mimbres Valley grow most of the Chenin Blanc grapes. Wines produced from this excellent white grape can vary from fresh, lively and fruity-light to dry, fine, full and aggressive. This wine complements poultry or pork dishes.

French-American Hybrids

Northern New Mexico is well suited to the growing of these varieties. Both reds and whites generally tend to be soft and especially pleasant to drink young. A red that has developed a fine bouquet with cask and bottle is the Marechal Foch.

French Colombard

This very prolific and vigorously growing white grape excels in New Mexico. Because of its high-acid juice, it is used in making white wines and champagnes, and it is a principal white wine grape in the Mesilla Valley. Blended with other white wines, it produces various light semi-sweet wines. French Colombard goes well with appetizers, Monterey Jack cheese or chicken, and it can be served as a dessert wine.

Merlot

Widely grown in the Mimbres Valley, Merlot is considered a premium red wine grape. Merlot ages faster and has a softer, more delicate character and less tannin than the Cabernet Sauvignon, and its flavor hints of plum, black cherry, violet and orange. Besides being a varietal wine, Merlot blends well with the Cabernet Sauvignon to make a fragrant, richly complex Bordeaux style wine. It is excellent served with wild fowl, beef and other heavy dishes as well as Camembert cheese and chocolate.

Muscat

Scores of different Muscat grapes are cultivated in southern New Mexico. All are spicy-flavored. Muscat of Alexandria and Muscat of Blanc produce a most delicious, sweet wine that is low in alcohol content. Muscat of Blanc, also known as Muscat Canelli, is primarily a dessert wine, while Muscat of Alexandria goes well with cheese, apples and pears.

Riesling

Also known as White Riesling, this grape produces some of New Mexico's most popular wines. It takes on a wide range of styles, from dry to sweet in the late harvest varieties. Aromas and flavors of apricots and melons characterize its bouquet. Riesling is excellent for dinner with seafood or poultry as well as with cheese and fruit. It can also be served with dessert.

Ruby Cabernet

These red grapes, which flourish in the Mesilla Valley, produce a powerful, astringent flavor, variously described as green olive, weedy and tannic. After being aged and bottled, Ruby Cabernet gradually loses its astringent taste and develops a fruity bouquet. It is an excellent wine to complement beef or spicy foods.

Sauvignon Blanc

Also known as Fume Blanc, Sauvignon Blanc has adapted well to New Mexico's climate and soils. This white wine grape produces a distinctive, grassy, herbaceous in character, dry white wine. Sauvignon Blanc is an excellent table wine to serve with seafood, fowl or vegetarian dishes.

Seyval Blanc

The most popular French hybrid white wine is Seyval Blanc. This delicately flavored wine goes well with poultry (especially turkey) and lighter seafood entrees.

Zinfandel

This big red grape is one of our most widely-planted varieties and produces large, tight bunches, sometimes more than the vine can handle. Aged in wood and bottled for several years, Zinfandel develops a fine bouquet. Zinfandel grapes produce a variety of wines from deep red to a pale rose to white. The red skins give the wine a robust flavor and color. When the skins are removed, the wine becomes pale or white, light and sweet. Gaining in popularity, these White Zinfandels are delightfully fresh and fruity with floral spicy aromas. They go well with cream sauces, fish, pork, and other lighter meals, including Asian and Latin foods. The more red in the wine the heartier the flavor. Red Zinfandel is a spicy, peppery wine with a hint of the fruity flavor of berries or dark cherries and is hearty enough to match up with beef, lamb, spicy foods and thick red sauces. All Zinfandels pair well with different types of cheeses.

Most of New Mexico's wineries are small to medium-sized operations. You can visit with the winemakers, who will be happy to let you sample their wines. Visiting these wineries or purchasing their wines at your local store gives you the flavor of New Mexico like nothing else. See pages 247–51 in the **Appendix** for detailed information about New Mexico wineries, including websites and contact information.

A Personal Note from the Author

The recipes I present here are intended to be used as guides only. Please feel free to modify the seasonings and flavors to suit your individual taste. You should not hesitate to experiment, once you learn the basics of preparing this cuisine. Use your imagination and make each special meal a celebration.

I have especially enjoyed the years since my first New Mexico cookbook was written. I have met many people who, like me, love New Mexico cuisine—wonderful folks who have been willing to share their recipes with me. A number of the recipes in this cookbook are the result of that sharing. It is my belief that recipes are to be shared and enjoyed.

I have long since lost track of the origin of most of those I have presented here. I have done my best to select recipes I consider special in one way or another. My hope is that you'll find them interesting, pleasing to your palate and worthy of your best effort. One thing is certain, you will never find New Mexico cuisine boring.

From the Land of Enchantment—*mucho gusto*!

Adios,

Clyde W. Casey
Roswell, New Mexico

# APPETIZERS

Appetite-creating foods are called *antojos* here. I get more requests for these taste-teasers than for any other menu items. A number of foods served as snacks or appetizers in New Mexico are regularly presented as main dishes in other states. Tacos, which are often found here as a snack as well as a main dish, are a typical example. Others are my **Green Chile Quiche**, which also makes a great first course dish, and my **Marinated Vegetables**, which make a nice side dish. Having a party? Want to warm up your guests? How about some **Chil-Eat-Zas**? Your guests will feel warm and welcome. **Guacamole** and **Chile Con Queso** are old standbys. There are almost as many different recipes for these two as there are cooks who make them. Here I offer my favorite versions. For a special taste treat, why not try a little cream cheese on a cracker or a tortilla chip topped with my **Green Chutney**? It's sure to please. **Shrimp Quesadillas** or **Potato Gordas** are both "winners" that might even help enhance your reputation as a great cook.

Our evenings are warm and pleasant, and a great many of us eat outdoors, enjoying the moderate climate. This offers an opportunity to serve appetizers and wine on the patio before dinner. In Santa Fe and many of our other cities, restaurants feature open-air dining. A fine wine, a tasty appetizer and enjoyable conversation make a delightful prelude to a memorable meal. Enjoy!

Ceviche

This raw fish dish is a popular appetizer in Mexico and is becoming more common in New Mexico. The fish looks and tastes as though it has been poached.

1 pound mild-flavored fish fillets (such as sole, halibut or whitefish)
¾ cup fresh lime juice (approx. 12 limes)
½ cup white onion, finely chopped
1 tablespoon canned New Mexico green chiles, chopped
1 teaspoon salt
3 small tomatoes, peeled, seeded and chopped
½ teaspoon dry-leaf oregano
3 tablespoons olive oil
2 tablespoons fresh cilantro, chopped
1 garlic clove, minced
¼ ground white pepper
¼ cup catsup

1. If fish has a skin, remove it. Slice fillets into thin strips. Place the strips in a glass dish or ceramic bowl and cover with lime juice. Refrigerate overnight.
2. Drain and add the remaining ingredients. Refrigerate for at least one hour, stirring occasionally. Can be used as dip.

Makes 4 servings.

Cheddar Chiles

When they are in season, I use red jalapeños. They have a richer, warmer taste than the green ones.

12 jalapeño chile peppers, seeded and halved
1 8-ounce package of cheddar cheese, cubed
1 cup all-purpose flour
1½ teaspoons ground red chile
4 eggs, beaten
1 cup fine, dry breadcrumbs
vegetable oil
ranch-style dressing

1. Process cheddar cheese in food processor until cheese has a moldable consistency.
2. Stuff jalapeños with processed cheese.
3. In a small bowl, beat eggs. In another bowl, place breadcrumbs.
4. In a shallow bowl, combine flour and ground chile. Stir well.
5. Dip stuffed chiles in beaten eggs. Dredge in flour mixture. Dip coated chiles back in egg again: dredge in bread crumbs, pressing so that crumbs will adhere.
6. Place prepared chiles on a wax-paper lined baking sheet and freeze for at least 30 minutes.
7. Heat vegetable oil in deep skillet until it reaches a temperature of 375ºF (190ºC). Fry chiles until golden brown. Drain on paper towels. Serve immediately with ranch dressing,

Makes 24.

Chil-Eat-Zas

Quick and easy to prepare—surprisingly good to eat.

1 pound lean ground beef
1 teaspoon vegetable oil
1 tube (10 count) refrigerator biscuits
1 7½-ounce can Mexican style tomato sauce
2 4-ounce cans New Mexico green chiles, drained
    OR 6 to 10 fresh or frozen green chiles, roasted, peeled, seeded,
    deveined and chopped
½ pound mozzarella cheese, sliced thin

1. In skillet, brown beef in a small amount of vegetable oil and drain.
    Set aside.
2. Preheat oven 300ºF (150ºC).
3. Separate biscuits and pat them out on a cookie sheet until they are
    flat circles. Spread tomato sauce on dough circles. Add layer of
    meat, then chiles and top with thin slices of cheese.
4. Bake for 15 to 20 minutes. Cut into quarters and serve hot.

Makes 40 appetizers.

Mozzarella cheese is a white cheese made from either whole or partially
skimmed milk. It has a firm texture and is usually available in sliced,
small round or shredded form. The "low moisture" varieties may have
preservatives added.

Chile Con Queso

Triple this recipe for your next party and keep it warm in a crockpot. Serve with flour tortillas or tortilla chips and watch it disappear.

2 tablespoons butter
½ medium onion, chopped
2 garlic cloves, minced
1 tablespoon all-purpose flour
⅓ cup chicken broth
2 fresh tomatoes, peeled
3 New Mexico green chiles, roasted, peeled, seeded, deveined and
    chopped
    OR 1 4-ounce can New Mexico green chiles, drained and chopped
¼ teaspoon ground cumin
fresh ground black pepper to taste
8 ounces Monterey Jack cheese, shredded or diced small
3 ounces cream cheese, diced small
½ cup heavy cream
warm flour tortillas (See p. 66.) or tortilla chips

1. Make sure cheeses are at room temperature.
2. In a food processor, combine tomatoes and chiles until they are chopped, but not pureed. Mix in cumin and black pepper.
3. In a small saucepan, melt butter. Cook onions and garlic until soft. Add tablespoon of flour and stir for one minute.
4. Add chile mixture to saucepan and cook over medium heat about 4 minutes. Add chicken broth and continue cooking until moisture has evaporated.
5. Remove the saucepan from the heat and stir in the cheese rapidly. When cheese is melted, add cream and thin to desired consistency. Do not overheat, or cheese will break down.
6. Serve with warm tortillas or tortilla chips.

Makes 4 appetizers.

Cream Cheese Chile Dip

This can be used as a spread or dip. It makes excellent stuffing for celery.

1 8-ounce package cream cheese
3 New Mexico green chiles, roasted, peeled, seeded, deveined and
    chopped
    OR 1 4-ounce can New Mexico green chiles, drained and chopped
2 tablespoons milk
1 tablespoon white onion, minced
garlic salt to taste

1. In a small bowl, combine all ingredients and beat until creamy, adding more milk as necessary.
2. Allow the dip to sit for at least one hour to allow the flavors to blend.

Makes 1 cup

Cream cheese is a mildly tangy, smooth, creamy-textured spreadable cheese. Developed in 1872, this soft unripened cheese is made from cows' milk. It is sometimes sold mixed with Neufchatel to lower butterfat content.

Green Chile Chutney

I use this chutney as an all-purpose breakfast sauce. It is especially good on **Blue Cornmeal Pancakes** (See p. 40.), biscuits and your breakfast eggs.

2 pounds Big Jim or New Mexico green chile of choice, roasted, peeled, deveined and chopped.
2 cups sugar
1 tablespoon roasted Mexican oregano
⅔ cup cider vinegar
1 teaspoon salt

1. Combine all ingredients and cook in non-stick skillet over medium heat 15 minutes.
2. Allow to cool and serve cold.

Makes 6 servings.

Piñon (pignolis or pine) nuts are harvested from the cone of the piñon pine tree. They are the largest non-cultivated crop in the USA. Although they are difficult to peel, there is no substitute for their sweet pine taste. The crop varies from year to year. They have been an important source of oil for American Indians for hundreds of years.

Green Chile Quiche

Here is a quiche with a sassy treatment. Serve it as an hors d'oeuvre or a first course with your favorite salsa.

Vegetable cooking spray
1 32-ounce package frozen "Southern Style" hash-brown potatoes, thawed
1 cup salsa
¼ cup ranch dressing
4 eggs, lightly beaten
1 cup milk
2 4-ounce cans New Mexico green chiles, diced
    OR 6 to 10 fresh or frozen green chiles, roasted, peeled, seeded, deveined and finely chopped
1 cup shredded Monterey Jack cheese
1 cup shredded cheddar cheese
sour cream
salsa
fresh cilantro

1. Preheat oven to 450ºF (230ºC). Spray a 13 x 9-inch baking dish with a vegetable cooking spray.
2. Line a large bowl with several layers of paper towels. Place the potatoes in a bowl and cover with 2 layers of paper towels, pressing to remove excess moisture.
3. Spread the potatoes evenly in bottom of prepared baking dish. Bake in preheated oven 45 minutes or until golden brown.
4. In a small bowl, blend salsa with ranch dressing. In another bowl, mix eggs and milk.
5. When potatoes are cooked, remove from oven. Reduce heat to 350ºF (175ºC). Spread salsa mixture over potatoes. Pour egg mixture over salsa.
6. Sprinkle chile peppers over eggs. Top with a layer of Monterey Jack cheese and then cheddar cheese.
7. Return to oven and bake 45 minutes or until cheese bubbles and is browned. Let stand 5 minutes before serving.
8. Top with each serving with sour cream, salsa and cilantro.

Makes 8 servings.

Guacamole

There are many recipes for guacamole, but this is my personal favorite. I use guacamole in many ways because it always adds special color, texture and taste.

2 ripe avocados
½ teaspoon salt
1 garlic clove, minced
1 teaspoon fresh lime juice
1 medium tomato, chopped
¼ cup white onion, finely chopped
1 jalapeño chile, minced
2 tablespoons fresh cilantro, chopped

1. Halve and pit avocados; place into glass or plastic bowl. Coarsely chop with two knives. Add salt and garlic, then lime juice, to taste.
2. Fold in tomato, onion, chile and cilantro. Allow flavors to blend for a few minutes before serving.

Makes 2 cups.

Although everyone seems to have a personal method for making guacamole, the real secret is ripe avocados. Your avacado is ripe if it yields to light thumb pressure.

Jalapeño Bean Dip

Why buy your dip from a market when it is this easy to prepare? Try it, and you will find there is no comparison in taste.

3 ripe jalapeños, seeded and minced
½ cup green onion, diced
1 cup fresh tomatoes, peeled and diced
2 cups **Refried Beans** (See p. 125.)
    OR 1 15-ounce can refried beans
1½ cups **Tomato Salsa** (See p. 194.)
    OR 1½ canned tomato salsa
½ cup black olives, pitted and sliced
1 cup cheddar cheese, shredded
tortilla chips

1. Preheat oven to 300ºF (150ºC).
2. In a bowl, combine all ingredients except ½ cup of the cheddar cheese. Mix well.
3. Place mixture in 8-inch baking dish. Sprinkle remaining ½ cup cheese on top. Bake 35 to 40 minutes.
4. Remove and place in serving dish. Serve with tortilla chips

Makes 6 servings.

Jalapeño chiles range from hot to very hot. Three inches long, they are green when immature and red when they ripen. Sold fresh, canned or pickled, they are the most famous chiles in the world.

Las Cruces Deviled Eggs

Here you go—deviled eggs with a sassy taste. Capers and cumin add interesting flavors.

12 cooked eggs, peeled
¼ cup mayonnaise
1 jalapeño pepper, seeded and finely chopped
1 tablespoon (or to taste) ground cumin
1 tablespoon capers, rinsed and finely chopped
1 tablespoon prepared mustard
½ teaspoon salt
⅛ teaspoon fresh ground black pepper
ground red chile powder
fresh cilantro, finely chopped

1. Cut eggs lengthwise into halves. Carefully slip out yolks into a small bowl; mash with fork. Stir in mayonnaise, jalapeño, cumin, capers, mustard, salt and black pepper, mix until smooth.
2. Fill egg halves with egg yolk mixture, heaping lightly. Sprinkle with red chile powder. Garnish with cilantro.

Makes 24 eggs.

Eggs are not only delicious as a food, but they are used as a leavening agent in breads, cakes and soufflés. Because they have been long maligned for their high cholesterol content, eggs are now becoming available in low cholesterol varieties in limited locations.

Layered Bean Dip

An attractive and economical party dish. Be sure to prepare a variety of vegetable sticks.

6 slices bacon, chopped
½ cup yellow onion, chopped
½ teaspoon ground red New Mexico chile
1 16-ounce can pinto beans, drained with ¼ cup liquid reserved
2 cups **Guacamole** (See p. 27.)
1 cup dairy sour cream
1 cup Colby or Monterey Jack cheese, shredded
¼ cup green onion chopped, including tops
cilantro
sliced ripe olives
tortilla chips
fresh vegetable sticks (jicama, carrot, zucchini, etc.)

1. In a medium skillet, sauté bacon, onions and ground chile until bacon is crisp.
2. In a large bowl, coarsely mash beans with fork and stir in the reserved liquid. Spread beans evenly into an 8-inch circle on serving platter.
3. Spread Guacamole over beans, then top with sour cream.
4. Sprinkle sour cream with cheese and green onions. Garnish with cilantro and olives.
5. Serve with tortilla chips and vegetables.

Makes 6 to 8 servings.

Marinated Vegetables

Every time I fix this dish I get rave reviews. Pretty as a picture, yet tasty, it is a sure winner.

10 cups water, divided
1 pound fresh peas
3 cups cauliflower florets
3 cups broccoli florets
1 cup carrots, diagonally sliced
1 yellow bell pepper, seeded and cut into ¼-inch strips
1 red bell pepper, seeded and cut into ¼-inch strips
6 Hungarian yellow wax peppers seeded and cut into rings

Marinade:
2 cups vinegar
¼ cup sugar
½ cup minced fresh basil
10 garlic cloves, minced
3 jalapeño peppers, seeded and minced
1 tablespoon whole pickling spices

1. In a 3-quart saucepan, bring 8 cups of water to a boil over high heat. Add peas, cauliflower, broccoli and carrots. Remove from heat and let stand for 1 minute.
2. Drain immediately, rinse under cold water and drain again. Transfer vegetables to a large bowl. Add bell and wax peppers and set aside.
3. In a 2-quart saucepan, combine remaining 2 cups water, vinegar and sugar; set aside.
4. Tie basil, garlic, minced jalapeño peppers and pickling spices in a cheesecloth bag; add to saucepan. Boil uncovered for 5 minutes. Remove from heat and cool; discard spice bag.
5. Pour cooled marinade over reserved vegetables and mix well. Cover and refrigerate for 24 hours.
6. Drain marinated vegetables and arrange on a serving platter.

Makes 8 servings.

Nachos

New Mexico's contribution to fast food. Nachos are one of the most popular foods sold in convenience stores across the nation.

1½ cups (6 ounces) cheddar cheese, shredded
6 jalapeño chiles, seeded and cut into slices
tortilla chips

1. Place tortilla chips on 4 small ovenproof dishes or a pie pan.
2. Sprinkle each with ¼ of the cheese and ¼ of the jalapeño slices.
3. Set oven to broil.
4. Broil about 3 to 4 inches from the heat until cheese is melted. Serve at once

Makes 4 servings.

These can also be prepared using a microwave or a toaster oven. Try garnishing them with lettuce, tomatoes, black olives, onions, or almost any vegetable. Sprinkle your selected garnish in and around the chips. Experiment with a variety of combinations.

Portales Spiced Peanuts

No one I know can eat just one of these. They are an ideal snack, so be prepared for them to disappear quickly.

2 teaspoons peanut oil
4 cloves garlic, crushed
2 cups unsalted dry-roasted Valencia red peanuts
2 tablespoons chili powder
½ teaspoon salt

1. In a large skillet heat oil over medium heat. Cook garlic, stirring occasionally until golden brown, then use strainer to remove garlic and return oil to pan. Discard garlic.
2. Add chili powder and peanuts and cook over medium heat for about 2 minutes, stirring occasionally, until peanuts are very warm. Remove peanuts and drain. While still warm sprinkle with salt. Cool.

Makes 2 cups.

Peanuts are an important cash crop in New Mexico. The peanut is actually a legume, not a nut; true nuts grow on trees. They are also called goobers, groundnuts or monkey nuts, because after flowering, the plant bends down to the earth and its pod ripens underground.

Potatoes Gordas

These fritters are a nice example of how New Mexicans combine chile, cheese and corn. Try them with my **Green Chile Stew** (See p. 57).

1 pound russet potatoes
3 New Mexico green chiles, roasted peeled, seeded and chopped
    OR 1 4-ounce can chopped New Mexico green chiles, drained
8 ounces cheddar cheese, grated
2 cups masa harina
1 teaspoon baking powder
1 cup water
½ teaspoon salt
oil for frying
sprigs of cilantro, for garnish

1. Scrub the potatoes and peel them or not, as desired. Cut them into chunks that are roughly the same size and steam or boil them in salted water until tender. Pass through a food mill or lightly break up with a fork.
2. In a medium mixing bowl, combine potatoes, chiles and cheddar cheese. Add masa harina, baking powder and salt. Add up to a cup of water slowly until mixture comes together.
3. Shape the dough into patties and fry on both sides in a generous amount of hot oil on a griddle or in a skillet until they are nicely browned. Drain on paper toweling and serve garnished with sprigs of cilantro.

Makes 4 to 6 servings.

Potato Skins with Green Chile

Having a party? These are a perfect treat!

8 small baking potatoes
vegetable oil
garlic salt
2 cups (8 ounces) shredded cheddar cheese
12 slices bacon, cooked and crumbled
2 tablespoons chopped fresh chives
1 8-ounce carton sour cream
2 tablespoons New Mexico green chiles, roasted, seeded and chopped.
⅛ teaspoon ground red chile

1. Preheat oven to 400°F (205°C).
2. Scrub potatoes and rub skins with vegetable oil. Prick each potato
    several times with a fork.
2. Place in oven and bake for 35 to 45 minutes or until done.
3. Allow potatoes to cool to touch. Cut top third of each potato;
    discard tops. Carefully scoop out pulp, leaving about ⅛-inch-thick
    shells. (Reserve pulp for other uses.)
4. Fry potato skins in hot—375°F (190°C)—oil for 3 to 4 minutes or
    until browned. Invert and drain on paper towels. Place potato skins,
    cut side up, on an ungreased baking sheet.
5. Sprinkle with garlic salt and cheddar cheese. Broil 6 inches from
    heat for 30 seconds or until cheese is melted. Top potato skins with
    crumbled bacon and 1 tablespoon of the chives.
6. In a small bowl, combine sour cream, chiles and ground red chile.
    Stir well. Top with the remaining chives. Serve with potato skins.

Makes 8 servings.

Shrimp Quesadillas

If you are looking for a special appetizer with a New Mexican touch, look no further. Seafood prepared Southwestern style is a real treat. Here is one of my favorite dishes.

4 tablespoons butter
4 10-inch flour tortillas
½ cup cheddar cheese, shredded
½ cup Monterey Jack cheese, shredded
2 jalapeño chiles, seeded, deveined and sliced
16 shrimp, shelled, cooked and sliced in half lengthwise
4 tablespoons dairy sour cream
1 large tomato, chopped
2 ripe avocados, peeled and sliced
paprika

1. Preheat oven to 350ºF (175ºC).
2. Lightly butter one side of 4 tortillas. Place tortillas, buttered side down, on a flat cookie sheet.
3. On each of the 4 tortillas, spread cheeses to within ¼-inch of edge. Place jalapeño slices and sliced shrimp on top.
4. Bake 6 to 8 minutes or until cheeses are melted and the tortillas start to brown slightly. Remove from oven and fold in half. Cut each half into three pieces.
5. Place pieces on serving plates. Garnish each piece with a dollop of sour cream. Arrange tomatoes and avocado slices over sour cream. Sprinkle with paprika.

Makes 4 servings.

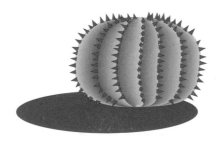

Stuffed Jalapeño Chile Peppers

If you can find the red-ripe jalapeño chiles, you are in for a treat. The mature pepper has a rich warm flavor. I fix these stuffed jewels as often as I can.

18 ripe red jalapeño chiles
1 8-ounce package cream cheese, softened
2 tablespoons lime juice
1 teaspoon ground cumin
1 teaspoon ground red New Mexico chile
dash fresh ground black pepper
2 tablespoons vegetable oil
½ cup chopped pecans
½ small white onion chopped
cilantro, finely chopped

1. Cut jalapeños in half lengthwise. Remove seeds and devein. Set aside.
2. In a medium bowl, combine all remaining ingredients except pecans, onions and cilantro. Beat with electric mixer until smooth.
3. Stir in pecans and onions. Stuff jalapenos with cream cheese mixture till slightly rounded. Cover and refrigerate at least 8 hours.
4. Serve sprinkled with cilantro.

Makes 36 stuffed chiles.

The next time you have party, prepare a full platter of these little red treats—a wonderful way to present the mature version of our most popular pepper. By doubling the recipe for the stuffing and adding a small can of corn nibblets, you will have a dip that will be a hit when served with chips.

BREAKFAST

Breakfast may be the simplest of all New Mexico cooking. Omelets, eggs and breakfast burritos in many forms are the main dishes. Breakfast burritos, consisting of warm, soft flour tortillas used to enclose typical fillings of eggs, sausage, bacon and potatoes, are by far our most popular breakfast food. They can be made in a variety of ways, starting with the simple **Breakfast Burrito**, an excellent way to start your day. For an unusual treat, whip up **Scrambled Eggs and Avocado** or try my **Baked Green Chile Omelet**. Both are sure to please. My personal favorite breakfast has to be **Blue Cornmeal Pancakes** (See p. 40) topped with my **Green Chile Chutney** (See p. 25).

Baked Green Chile Omelette

Here is a great way to start the day! A true New Mexico specialty!

¼ pound bacon, finely diced
1 6-ounce can cream-style corn
1 4-ounce can New Mexico green chiles, drained and chopped
    OR 3 to 5 fresh or frozen green chiles, roasted, peeled, seeded,
    deveined and chopped
1 teaspoon sugar
⅛ teaspoon garlic powder
3 tablespoons light cream
6 large eggs
1 cup cheddar cheese, grated
salt to taste

1. Preheat oven to 375ºF (190ºC). Butter an 8-inch baking dish; set
    aside.
2. Fry bacon and drain off excess grease.
3. Mix bacon with corn, chiles, sugar and garlic powder. Spread evenly
    in prepared dish.
4. In a bowl, combine cream, eggs and salt to taste. Pour over the
    corn-chile mixture. Sprinkle cheese evenly on top.
5. Place on center rack of preheated oven and bake 35 to 40 minutes,
    or until egg mixture is set. Fold over when serving.

Makes 6 servings.

Blue Cornmeal Pancakes

The heartier flavor of the blue cornmeal makes these pancakes unique and satisfying. The slate-blue color is impressive and different. Another true New Mexico specialty.

1 cup blue corn masa or blue cornmeal
½ cup all-purpose flour
1 tablespoon sugar
2 teaspoons baking powder
½ teaspoon salt
3 tablespoons dry milk powder
2 eggs
1¼ cups milk
2 tablespoons vegetable oil

1. Sift together the dry ingredients into a mixing bowl. In a separate bowl, beat eggs; add milk and oil and blend well. The batter will be a little thin.
2. Heat griddle over medium heat. Brush with a small amount of oil and cook pancakes at preferred size.
3. Serve pancakes hot.
4. Serve with **Green Chile Chutney** (See p. 25.) or your choice of pancake toppings.

Makes 4 servings.

Corn is the New World's single most important contribution to the human diet. Only wheat acreage surpasses corn in number of acres planted. Columbus brought back corn with him to Europe, and within a generation it was being grown throughout southern Europe.

Breakfast Burritos

The burrito, once a mainstay only in New Mexico cooking, has become a popular fast food nationwide. I first became a burrito fan as a young man, when I worked on a ranch in eastern Colorado and we had a Spanish lady who cooked for us. There are as many varieties of burritos as there are cooks who make them. I particularly like this one for a fast, easy breakfast. A great way to start the day.

5 slices bacon
1 tablespoon butter
4 eggs, beaten
salt
salsa of choice
4 softened warm flour tortillas (See p. 66.)

1. Place bacon between two paper towels on a paper plate. Cook in microwave 4–5 minutes, just until bacon is crisp. Break into pieces.
2. Melt butter in skillet. Scramble eggs until almost done. Add bacon. Cook 30 seconds to 1 minute. Salt to taste.
3. Heat salsa in small pan until very hot.
4. Spoon egg mixture equally into center of softened warm flour tortillas. Coat with salsa and fold burrito-style. Serve immediately.

Makes four burritos.

Green Chiles & Chipped Beef

One of my favorites, this dish takes a little time to prepare but it's worth the effort. For an option, you can use diced ham instead of chipped beef.

1 tablespoon butter
1 garlic clove, minced
¼ pound chipped beef, chopped
½ pound fresh mushrooms, diced
1 cup New Mexico green chiles, diced
1 cup sour cream
1 tablespoon, dried parsley
½ teaspoon dried leaf oregano
6 large eggs
salt
fresh ground black pepper, to taste
¾ cup grated cheddar cheese
sliced black olives for garnish

1. Preheat oven to 350ºF (175ºC).
2. In a skillet melt the butter. Add garlic and chipped beef and sauté for two minutes. Add mushrooms and green chiles and sauté for two more minutes.
3. Remove from heat and stir in sour cream, parsley and oregano. Let stand for 10 minutes to blend flavors, then turn into a buttered one quart casserole dish.
4. With a tablespoon make six rounded hollows in the chile mixture. Break egg into each hollow. Season with salt and black pepper.
5. Place in oven and bake for about 20 minutes or until egg whites are set. Remove from oven and sprinkle grated cheese over casserole mixture. Return to oven and bake until cheese is bubbling.
6. Garnish with sliced olives.

Makes 6 servings.

Huevos Rancheros

Huevos rancheros means "eggs ranch-style" or "eggs country-style" in Spanish. This dish is usually served as a mid-morning breakfast, or *almuerzo*, on rural farms where Hispanic workers have a much smaller meal at dawn. The traditional version of huevos rancheros consists of corn tortillas, fried lightly, and fried eggs with a hot tomato/chili sauce. Nowadays, commercially prepared salsa and flour tortillas are often used to make this quick morning breakfast very easy to prepare, but I still prefer to use corn tortillas.

4 corn tortillas
cooking oil
4 eggs
1 cup of salsa of choice
pinch of chili powder
chopped green chile peppers to taste
¼ white onion, chopped
1 cup refried beans
Monterey Jack cheese, to taste
sliced, ripe avocado

1. Pre-heat oven to 500°F (260°C). Coat each tortilla in oil and place on cookie sheet. Cook for approximately 5-10 minutes, depending on how crisp you prefer your tortillas.
2. Heat dash of oil in a frying pan over medium low heat. Cook each egg slowly on one side until whites are firm and yolks are still runny. Salt to taste.
3. Place one egg on each tortilla.
4. Heat salsa in small pan on high heat for about 2 minutes or until extremely hot. Add chili powder and chopped chiles. Pour ¼ cup over the top of each egg. Heat of salsa will further cook the top of the egg.
5. Let sit for about 1 minute before serving. Spread chopped onion and shredded cheese over the top, and serve with sliced avocado and refried beans.

Makes 4 servings.

Scrambled Eggs and Avocados

This is the first recipe that I tried with cooked avocados. If you have never had cooked avocado, give this one a try.

2 medium-sized avocados, seeded, peeled and chopped
1 tablespoon lemon juice
1 medium white onion, minced
1 4-ounce can New Mexico green chiles, drained and chopped
    OR 3 to 5 fresh or frozen green chiles, roasted, peeled, seeded, deveined and chopped
6 eggs, slightly beaten
4 tablespoons butter
¼ teaspoon ground red chile
salt to taste

1. Place avocados in a small bowl and sprinkle with lemon juice. Set aside.
2. In a large skillet, melt butter, then add onions and sauté until soft. Add avocados and cook for two minutes. Add chiles and cook for an additional two minutes.
3. Add beaten eggs, season with ground chiles and salt. Do not overcook!

Makes 4 servings.

Vaquero Breakfast

Hard work requires a hearty breakfast. This one fills the bill if you are looking for a solid New Mexico way to start the day.

3 medium Russet potatoes
4 8-inch flour tortillas
1 teaspoon butter
2 cups chili (homemade or commercial—try my **Bowl of Red**, p. 132.)
4 large eggs
1 cup ripe tomatoes, chopped
½ cup sliced green onions, with a few tops
½ cup cheddar cheese, shredded
1 cup salsa of choice
salt to taste

1. Preheat oven to 400ºF (205ºC).
2. Cook, peel and dice potatoes
3. Rub both sides of tortillas with butter and place into 2 loaf pans (2 tortillas per pan). Gently shape each to create a bowl.
4. In a medium saucepan, heat chili. Stir in pre-cooked potatoes and cook until thoroughly heated.
5. Divide chili and place on shaped tortillas. With back of tablespoons, make an indentation in each chili mixture.
6. Break egg into each indentation. Bake 5 minutes. Cover loosely with foil. Bake 5 to 10 minutes longer or until eggs are done.
7. Gently lift each bowl from loaf pan and place on serving plate. Spoon on tomatoes and onions. Sprinkle with cheese. Serve with salsa.

Makes 4 servings.

SALADS & SOUPS

For years I have looked for a potato salad with a New Mexico flair. Recently, I found a great one—**Peppery Potato Salad**—and I want to share it with you. This colorful, tasty creation is a sure hit that you will prepare again and again. It is easy to fix and can be made ahead of time. For a different salad why not try **Taos Black-eyed Pea Salad**. This combination of jicama, red bell peppers, zucchini and black-eyed peas is not only great eating, but it makes a beautiful presentation, looking as good as it tastes.

With soups, some like them hot and some like them cool. I love the aroma of a steaming pot of homemade soup. If you like hot, try my **Green Chile Stew** or **Meatball Soup with Vegetables**, sure to warm you on a cold night. For a cool treat, the **Santa Fe Gazpacho** is a refreshingly cold, summertime soup, or try the **Chilled Squash Soup**, low in fat and yet full and rich tasting. Both of these dishes are old standards here in the Land of Enchantment. Some of these soups are meals in themselves.

SALADS

Jalapeño Pasta Salad

An attractive salad that is low in fat and easy to fix. It tastes as good as it looks.

1⅓ cups bow-tie pasta (farfalle)
½ cup nonfat yogurt
1 tablespoon Dijon mustard
½ teaspoon salt
3 Roma tomatoes, cut lengthwise in half and sliced
2 green onions, cut diagonally into ½-inch pieces
2 jalapeno chiles seeded and finely minced
1 large garlic clove, minced
lettuce leaves

1. Cook pasta as directed on package; drain. Rinse with cold water; drain.
2. In large bowl mix pasta and remaining ingredients except lettuce. Cover and refrigerate until chilled. Serve on lettuce leaves.

Makes 6 servings.

If your luck is running out at the horse track in Ruidoso, try Deming, New Mexico. The Great American Duck Races are held each year in late August. Besides fast-feathered quacky races, you will find dancing and hot-air balloon races, as well as a tortilla toss, a craft show and flea market.

Jicama Salad

The nutty, slightly sweet taste and crisp texture of the jicama are complemented by citrus fruits, creating a fresh light flavor.

2 medium jicamas
2 oranges
2 limes
¼ cup golden raisins
1 tablespoon sunflower seeds, chopped
¼ teaspoon salt
2 teaspoons mint leaves, chopped
lettuce leaves
dash of chili powder

Dressing:
liquid from salad
1 tablespoon vegetable oil
2 tablespoons plain nonfat yogurt

1. Using a sharp knife, remove thick outer brown peel of jicama. Cut into bite size pieces, making about 2 cups.
2. Peel oranges and remove seeds and membranes. Slice into thin slices. Juice limes.
3. In a bowl, combine the jicama, orange slices, ½ of the lime juice, raisins, sunflower seeds, salt and mint leaves. Refrigerate for several hours.
4. Remove from refrigerator and bring to cool room temperature.
5. Make dressing: Drain excess liquid into small bowl, add reserved lime juice and dressing ingredients and stir well. Pour over salad and toss to coat.
5. Serve on bed of leaf lettuce. Sprinkle with a dash of chili powder.

Makes 6 servings.

Peppery Potato Salad

This is the one for your Fourth of July celebration. It travels well, and it is a crowd-pleaser.

3 pounds red potatoes, peeled and cut into ½-inch-thick slices
2 tablespoons white wine-vinegar
1 yellow bell pepper, seeded and cut into 1½-inch julienne strips
1 red bell pepper, seeded and cut into 1½-inch julienne strips
3 New Mexican chiles, roasted, peeled, seeded and cut into 1½-inch
    julienne strips
3 to 5 fresh or frozen green chiles, roasted, peeled, seeded, deveined
    OR 1 4-ounce can chopped New Mexico green chiles, drained,
    cut into 1½-inch julienne strips
½ cup minced green onions with tops
⅓ cup fresh parsley, minced
1 tablespoon drained capers
Lettuce leaves
Tomato wedges

Hot Salsa Mayonnaise Dressing:
2 cloves garlic, crushed
¼ cup reduced-calorie mayonnaise
⅓ cup commercial hot salsa
1 tablespoon sweet pickle relish

1. First make Hot Salsa Mayonnaise Dressing. Combine all ingredients in a small bowl; mix well. Cover and refrigerate 1 hour or until thoroughly chilled.
2. Cut potato slices in half and place in a 3-quart saucepan. Cover with water, and bring to a boil. Boil 4 to 5 minutes or until tender. Drain immediately and transfer to a large bowl.
3. Sprinkle potatoes with vinegar and toss to coat.
4. Add peppers, green onions, parsley, capers and Hot Salsa Mayonnaise Dressing to potatoes; stir well. Cover and chill thoroughly. Serve on lettuce leaves. Garnish with tomato wedges.

Makes 8 servings.

Taos Black-Eyed Pea Salad

Attractive, colorful, tasty—what more could you want in a salad?

2 10-ounce packages frozen black-eyed peas
1 medium jicama
1 medium zucchini
2 cups water
¼ cup chopped fresh cilantro
1 red bell pepper coarsely chopped
6 lettuce leaves

Dressing:
⅓ cup lemon juice
1 teaspoon sugar
½ teaspoon chili powder
½ teaspoon cumin
⅛ teaspoon ground red New Mexico chile
½ teaspoon garlic clove, minced
2 teaspoons vegetable oil

1. In a 2-quart saucepan, bring water to a boil; add black-eyed peas and reduce heat to low. Cover; cook 18–22 minutes until black-eyed peas are tender. Drain; rise with cold water. Cool 5 minutes.
2. Using sharp knife, remove brown peel of jicama. Rinse and cut into 1½ x ¼-inch sticks. Peel and cut zucchini into 1½ x ¼-inch sticks. Set aside.
3. In a large bowl, combine black-eyed peas and remaining salad ingredients except lettuce.
4. In a small bowl, whisk together all dressing ingredients. Pour over salad and toss well. Serve warm or chilled on lettuce leaves.

Makes 6 servings.

Tostada Salad

A refreshing salad that is a complete meal in itself. I like the contrast of the cold shredded lettuce, warm filling and melted cheese.

6 8-inch flour tortillas
3 tablespoons butter, melted
1 pound lean ground beef
1 teaspoon ground red New Mexico chile
¼ teaspoon ground cumin
¼ teaspoon dried-leaf oregano
¼ teaspoon garlic powder
¼ teaspoon onion powder
⅛ teaspoon freshly ground black pepper
½ cup tomato sauce
½ cup water
2 cups shredded lettuce
1 15.5-ounce can kidney beans, drained
1 large tomato, seeded, chopped
1 small white onion, chopped
½ cup ripe black olives, sliced
½ cup avocado, peeled, seeded and diced
1 8-ounce jar jalapeño flavored pasteurized processed cheese spread, melted
Dairy sour cream

1. Preheat oven to 350ºF (175ºC). Lightly brush melted butter on each side of tortillas. Place tortillas on cookie sheets. Bake 10 to 12 minutes or until dry, crisp and lightly browned. Set aside.
2. In a large skillet, brown ground beef; drain. Add seasonings, tomato sauce and water. Simmer for 5 minutes, stirring occasionally.
3. To assemble, place baked tortillas on serving plates. Top each with warm meat mixture, lettuce, beans, tomato, onion, olives and avocado. Pour melted cheese over salads.
4. Serve with sour cream.

Makes 6 servings.

West of the Pecos Pasta Salad

Colorful and tasty, this is a great use of tomatillos.

3 cups tricolor pasta spirals
1 20-ounce can pineapple chunks
6 fresh tomatillos
½ jalapeño chile, seeded and chopped
2 tablespoons canola oil
1 tablespoon fresh cilantro, chopped
½ teaspoon grated lime peel
¼ teaspoon salt

1. Cook pasta as directed on package; drain and rinse with cold water; drain.
2. Drain pineapple, reserving 2 tablespoons of juice.
3. Remove husks from fresh tomatillos and cut each into 8 wedges.
4. In a serving bowl, mix pasta, tomatillos, chile and pineapple.
5. In a small bowl, mix reserved pineapple juice and remaining ingredients. Pour over pasta mixture; toss. Cover and refrigerate at least 2 hours until chilled.

Makes 6 servings.

Tomatillos are fat little vegetables slightly larger than cherry tomatoes. They grow in papery husks reminiscent of Japanese lanterns and taste best when they are brilliant green in color. By the time they begin to turn yellow, they have lost some of their acid freshness. Select tomatillos with their husks still drawn tightly around them. Husk and rinse off the sticky residue before using them.

SOUPS

Beef & Green Chile Soup

This is one of my favorite soups. Adjust the heat by the number and type of green chiles you use. Another variation calls for the use of chorizo sausage instead of ground beef (again adjusting chiles accordingly).

1½ pounds lean ground beef
1 large white onion, chopped
2 large garlic cloves, minced
1 1.25-ounce package taco seasoning mix
1 28-ounce can whole tomatoes, undrained and chopped.
2 16-ounce cans red kidney beans, drained
1 15-ounce can tomato sauce
1 10½-ounce can beef broth, slightly diluted
2 4-ounce cans New Mexico green chiles, drained and chopped
    OR 6 to 10 fresh or frozen green chiles, roasted, peeled, seeded,
    deveined and chopped
3 tablespoons of jalapeño chiles, seeded and chopped.
½ cup water
1 teaspoon ground cumin
1 teaspoon ground red chile
1 cup chopped fresh tomato
1 cup shredded cheddar cheese
corn chips

1. In a 6-quart Dutch oven or heavy pot, brown beef. Add onion and garlic; cook until soft. Drain well and return to pot.
2. Add taco seasoning mix; stir well. Add chopped canned tomatoes and next 8 ingredients. Bring to a boil. Cover, reduce heat and simmer 30 minutes.
3. Garnish bowls of soup with chopped tomatoes, shredded cheese and corn chips.

Makes 15 cups.

Black Bean Chicken Soup

Black beans are now readily available, and you will find them an interesting treat in this unusual soup.

1 tablespoon olive oil
1 large onion, chopped
1 clove garlic, chopped
2 14-ounce cans chicken broth
1 14- or 15-ounce can black beans, rinsed and drained
2 4-ounce cans New Mexico green chiles, undrained and chopped
    OR 6 to 10 fresh or frozen green chiles, roasted, peeled, seeded,
    deveined and chopped
2 teaspoons dried-leaf oregano, crushed
1½ teaspoons ground cumin
1 teaspoon garlic powder
¼ teaspoon ground cloves
¼ teaspoon ground red chile
3 cups cooked chicken, diced
Low-fat cheddar cheese, shredded (optional)

1. In a 4-quart Dutch oven or heavy pot, heat olive oil; add onion and garlic; cook until soft.
2. Add remaining ingredients, except for chicken and cheese.
3. Bring to a boil and reduce heat, cover and simmer for 20 minutes, stirring occasionally.
4. Add chicken and cook covered, about 10 minutes or until heated through.
5. If desired, serve with cheese sprinkled on top.

Makes 4 servings.

Chilled Squash Soup

This cool and colorful soup has a snappy taste. The jalapeño pepper lends a delightful contrast to the mild squash.

2 tablespoons margarine
2 garlic cloves, minced
1 medium onion, chopped
1 jalapeño chile, cut into rings and seeded
2 teaspoons sugar
1½ teaspoons curry powder
½ teaspoon dry mustard
¼ teaspoon ground allspice
4 cups water
1½ teaspoons chicken-flavored bouillon granules
1/3 cup uncooked regular rice
4 medium yellow squash, sliced
1 8-ounce carton plain nonfat yogurt
2 tablespoons fresh lime juice
¼ cup green onions, minced

1. In a 6-quart saucepan, melt margarine. Add garlic and sauté 1 minute or until tender.
2. Add onion and jalapeno pepper; stir well. Add sugar, curry powder, mustard and allspice. Cook 4 to 5 minutes over medium heat, stirring constantly.
3. Add water, bouillon granules, rice and sliced yellow squash to vegetable mixture and bring to boil. Cover, reduce heat and simmer 20 to 30 minutes or until rice is tender.
4. In a blender or food processor, blend ½ of the cooked mixture. Repeat process with remaining mixture.
5. Pour into a large bowl. Cover and refrigerate 12 hours or overnight.
6. To serve, stir yogurt and lime juice into chilled soup. Top with minced green onions.

Makes 6 Servings.

Green Chile Corn Soup

If you have never eaten corn soup, give this one a try.

6 tomatillos
2 cups water
3½ cups frozen corn, thawed
1 cup chicken stock
¼ cup butter
3 cups milk
1 clove garlic, minced
1 tablespoon fresh oregano minced or 1 teaspoon dried dry-leaf oregano
1 4-ounce can New Mexico green chiles, drained and chopped
    OR 3 to 5 fresh or frozen green chiles, roasted, peeled, seeded,
    deveined and chopped
salt and pepper to taste
1 whole chicken breast, cooked, boned and chopped
1 cup fresh tomatoes, diced
1 cup Monterey Jack cheese, grated
fresh cilantro leaves, coarsely chopped for garnish
salt and fresh ground black pepper

1. Remove the papery husks from the tomatillos and rinse them. In a
   small saucepan, bring 2 cups of water to boil then lower the heat to
   a simmer. Drop the tomatillos into the simmering water and cook
   slowly for 10 minutes. Pour the mixture into a blender and puree.
   Set aside.
2. Combine corn and chicken stock in the blender and puree. Remove
   and set aside.
3. In a 4-quart Dutch oven or heavy pot, combine butter, the corn
   mixture and the tomatillo puree. Simmer slowly for 5 minutes,
   stirring occasionally.
4. Add milk, garlic, oregano, salt, chiles and pepper. Bring to a boil,
   reduce heat and simmer for 5 minutes.
5. Add chicken and tomatoes. Bring to a boil again then remove from
   heat. Add cheese and stir until melted. Garnish with cilantro.
6. Salt and pepper to taste.

Makes 4 servings

Green Chile Stew

Traditional in many homes, this is one of the first truly New Mexican dishes I learned to make.

2 pounds boneless pork, cut into 1-inch cubes
3 tablespoons all-purpose flour
2 tablespoons butter
1 cup white onion, chopped
2 garlic cloves, minced
3 cups ripe tomatoes, peeled, chopped
1 teaspoon salt
½ teaspoon dried-leaf oregano
¼ teaspoon ground cumin
water as necessary
20 fresh New Mexico green chiles, roasted, peeled, seeded, deveined and
    chopped
    OR 4 4-ounce cans of New Mexico green chile, chopped.

1. Toss pork with flour to coat. In a 4-quart Dutch oven or heavy pot,
    heat butter and add pork cubes a few at a time. Stir to brown. Push
    to side of pot and add onion and garlic. Cook until onion is soft.
    Stir in browned pork.
2. Add tomatoes, salt, oregano and cumin. Cover and simmer 1 hour,
    adding water as necessary and stirring occasionally. Add chiles,
    simmer 30 minutes more and continue adding water as necessary.

Makes 4 servings.

Hopi Lamb Stew

Still used today, this old stew recipe is a nice way to enjoy lamb. Sheep production is still very important to the Hopi Indians. I learned how to make this stew from a sheepherder in the early 1960s.

4 pounds lamb shoulder, bone in
6 quarts water
1 white onion, quartered
2 garlic cloves, chopped
6 juniper berries, crushed
1 teaspoon salt
½ teaspoon black peppercorns
½ teaspoon dried sage leaves
1 26-ounce can hominy, rinsed and drained
½ cup onion, finely chopped for garnish
1 4-ounce can New Mexico green chiles, drained and finely chopped
    OR 3 to 5 fresh or frozen green chiles, roasted, peeled, seeded,
    deveined and finely chopped for garnish

1. Trim fat and connective tissue from lamb shoulder. Place in large stockpot and cover with 4 inches of cold water.
2. Bring to boil; lower heat to medium. Skim fat as needed. Add water as needed to keep water level 3 inches above meat. Simmer uncovered for 1 hour.
3. Add onion, garlic, juniper berries, salt, peppercorns and sage to pot. Simmer covered 1 hour longer, skimming if needed.
4. Strain broth through cloth-lined colander into another pot. Remove vegetables, herbs and spices. Cut up the meat, removing the bone, and return it to the strained broth. Add hominy and simmer, covered, for 30 minutes. Serve hot with onions and chile as garnish.

Makes 6 servings.

Meatball Soup with Vegetables

I first tasted this soup when we moved here. It is a New Mexico dish that is little known outside this state.

Meatballs:
½ pound chuck steak, cut into small pieces
½ pound pork shoulder, cut into small pieces
⅔ cup dry bread crumbs
1 egg
⅓ cup milk
1 teaspoon salt
1 teaspoon ground coriander
1 teaspoon dried-leaf oregano, crushed
¼ teaspoon fresh ground black pepper
¼ cup canned New Mexico green chiles, chopped
    OR 2 fresh or frozen New Mexico green chiles, roasted, peeled,
    seeded, deveined and chopped
¼ medium white onion, coarsely chopped
2 garlic cloves, chopped
1 dried chipotle chile, stemmed, seeded and chopped

Broth and vegetables:
2 cups beef broth
2 cups chicken broth
½ cup each of turnips, zucchini, peeled carrots, all cut into thin 2-inch
    strips
¼ cup fresh cilantro, chopped

1. In a food processor or blender, process meat until coarse ground.
2. In a bowl, combine bread crumbs, egg and milk, stirring with fork to moisten the crumbs. Add the meat and the remaining ingredients. Process until the mixture is smooth.
3. Shape mixture into small meatballs. Use 1 tablespoon for each ball. Brown meatballs in a skillet then set aside.
4. In a 4-quart saucepan combine broths and bring to a boil. Drop in meatballs and cook for 5 minutes. Add vegetables, cover and simmer for 10 minutes.

Serve immediately, garnished with cilantro.

Makes 6 servings.

Menudo

Traditionally served on Christmas or New Years Eve, Menudo is a soup consisting mainly of corn in some form and tripe. Nowadays canned hominy is most often used. Said to be a cure for hangovers, it is frequently served in all-night cafes.

5 pounds tripe
1 large veal knuckle
4 large cloves garlic, minced
1 tablespoon salt
2 cups white onion, chopped
1 teaspoon fresh cilantro, minced
1 4-ounce can New Mexico green chiles, chopped
    OR 3 to 5 fresh or frozen green chiles, roasted, peeled, seeded,
    deveined and chopped
4 quarts water
1 1-pound 13-ounce can hominy, drained
2 tablespoons lemon juice
2 cups green onion, some with green tops, chopped
1½ cups fresh mint, chopped

1. Prepare tripe. Rinse under cold water. Place in a saucepan with enough water to cover and let stand for 2 hours. Remove and cut into 1/4 inch strips or slivers. Rinse once more with cold water for an additional 5 minutes.
2. Drain cut tripe stripes and place in an 8-quart kettle or Dutch oven.
3. Add veal knuckle, garlic, salt, onion, cilantro, green chiles and water. Cover and simmer for about 6 or 7 hours or until the tripe is fork tender. Add more water as needed.
4. Remove and discard the veal knuckle. Add hominy and heat until hot throughout. Add lemon juice.

Serve with green onion and mint sprinkled on top of each individual serving bowl.

Makes 8 to 10 main dish servings.

Potato Soup

Here's a favorite of the 1940s that is still served in Roswell and represents the ranch style cooking that is a part of any authentic New Mexico recipe collection.

4 tablespoons butter
6 to 8 green onions, sliced thin
¼ cup parsley, chopped
6 potatoes, peeled and diced
4 bouillon cubes
4½ cups water
¼ cup milk
¾ teaspoon celery salt
1¼ teaspoon salt
¼ teaspoon ground black pepper
2 eggs, hard-boiled, sliced thin
3 strips bacon, fried crisp, chopped

1. In a Dutch oven or heavy pot, heat butter and add green onions. Include part of the green tops. Cook slowly until tender.
2. Add parsley, potatoes, bouillon cubes and water. Cook until potatoes are soft.
3. Force mixture through a coarse sieve into large bowl.
4. Return to Dutch oven. Add milk and seasonings and heat thoroughly. Serve garnished with eggs and bacon.

Makes 6 servings.

Santa Fe Gazpacho

Santa Fe has numerous outdoor restaurants, and this is a popular mid-day lunch in this enchanting city. I also like it served with sourdough bread.

1 white onion diced
3 garlic cloves, minced
½ teaspoon salt
1 tablespoon extra virgin olive oil
5 cups vegetable stock, divided
9 ripe tomatoes, cored
1 cucumber, trimmed and peeled
1 jalapeño chile, seeded and diced
2 New Mexico green chiles, roasted, seeded, deveined and diced
1 red bell pepper, seeded and diced
2 tablespoons minced parsley
2 tablespoons minced cilantro
¼ cup lemon juice
2 tablespoons lime juice
salt and fresh ground pepper to taste
16 or more lettuce leaves
16 slices dry French bread, broken up

1. In a medium skillet, heat olive oil. Add onion and garlic; cook until onions are soft.
2. Transfer to a blender and add salt and 3 cups vegetable stock. Blend until smooth and pour into large bowl.
3. Place tomatoes, cucumber and 2 cups of stock into a blender and blend. This may be done in two batches. Add mixture to onion stock mixture in large bowl.
4. Add remaining minced vegetables, herbs and juices to soup. Season to taste with salt and freshly ground black pepper.
5. Cover and refrigerate 1 hour before serving. To serve line deep bowls or stemmed glasses with lettuce leaves. Add soup and bread in layers and serve with long-handled spoons.

Makes 6 to 8 servings.

BREADS

Tortillas are the mainstay of New Mexican breads, but the Western ranching influence is very strong here. Sourdough and fruit breads are always welcome.

I love the taste and smell of fresh baked goods. I remember the aroma of my Aunt Tiny's baked bread, fresh from her old wood-burning stove. It's been many years since I last sat down at her table for a lunch of oven-warm potato bread, hand churned-butter, sweet onions and cold fresh milk.

From **Bread of the Dead** to **Sweet Saffron Rolls**, I present here a varied and palate-pleasing assortment of breads, biscuits and muffins. Some are old favorites like **New Mexican Sweet Bread** and **Spiced Pumpkin Bread**. Some are new, such as **Sourdough Blue Cornmeal Bread** and **Ranch Buttermilk Bran Muffins**. All are recipes that are sure to please.

I realize that it is easier to go to the supermarket and take coffeecake or bread off the shelf, but then you miss that special smell and taste of homemade baked goods.

High altitude baking: Altitude can have an effect on cooking, particularly baking. For a discussion of baking at high altitudes, see "Altitude Adjustments" on pages 241–43 in the Appendix.

Tortillas—The Southwest Bread of Life

The tortilla is the mainstay of New Mexican breads and historically essential to the diet of Southwestern peoples. With no refrigeration, the use of dry food during the winter months was critical to the Indians' survival. Corn, because it stores well and is quickly ground, was ideal. The corn was ground into masa and shaped by hand into flat, round, thin pancakes. These were used as food holders, scoops and wrappers for a variety of recipes using peppers, corn and beans. Today, an endless variety of recipes—tacos, burritos, chimichangas, enchiladas, quesadillas, flautas and tostadas—all begin with tortillas, combined with sauces, salsas, and toppings; they are the heart and soul of New Mexican cuisine.

Corn tortillas are fried until crisp and can be stacked, rolled, folded, torn, cut and crumbled, making them among our most versatile of breads. Flour tortillas are often served as bread in a steamy hot form, often in a moist napkin or insulated container to keep them as warm as possible. Here in New Mexico, we sometimes use tortillas as a substitute for eating utensils—using them as plates, bowls or scoops. Today, an endless variety of recipes depend on these little thin cakes of corn or flour.

Corn tortillas are made from *masa harina* (dehydrated masa flour). Making corn tortillas by hand is an art, but nowadays they are readily available—freshly made or frozen—in most supermarkets. If you wish to make your own, you might consider a tortilla press, which is easy to use and inexpensive. Without a press, pat or roll the masa harina dough into a circular shape—usually about 6 inches in diameter—and trim until evenly round.

Flour tortillas are also available freshly made or frozen in many supermarkets. They can also be made in your kitchen using an all-purpose flour dough and a rolling pin to flatten. They are generally slightly larger (about 8 inches in diameter) than the corn variety.

Frozen tortillas have a long life and should be thawed before reheating. Those that aren't frozen should be stored in the refrigerator and covered in order to retain their flavor and keep from drying out. For those of you who wish to make your own, here are some recipes:

Corn Tortillas

2 cups masa harina flour
1½ cups warm water

1. Mix masa flour with enough warm water to make dough hold together.
2. Shape dough with your hands into a smooth ball. Divide dough into 12 equal pieces, and shape each piece into a ball.
3. If you have a tortilla press, place each dough ball on wax paper and hand press slightly. Then place a second piece of wax paper on top. Place wax paper-covered dough in press and push down. Cover and refrigerator until ready for use.
4. If you use a rolling pin, place dough ball between two pieces of cloth that have been dipped in water and wrung out. Roll ball of dough out with light, even strokes, turning until shape is a circle about 6 inches in diameter. Carefully pull back cloth and trim to a round circle, if necessary. Cover and refrigerate until ready for use.
5. Place shaped tortilla on preheated, dry, heavy griddle or heavy frying pan that has been heated over medium heat to approximately 350ºF (175ºC).
6. Cook until dry around the edge, about 1½ minutes. Turn over and repeat process until tortilla is dry, about 2 minutes.
7. Stack tortillas, placing wax paper between each, then cover with damp towel.
8. May be served hot or wrapped in foil and stored in refrigerator.

Makes 12 tortillas.

Flour Tortillas

3 cups all-purpose flour
2 teaspoons baking powder
¾ teaspoon salt
about 1 cup warm water
3 to 4 tablespoons lard or shortening

1. Sift together flour, baking powder and salt. Cut in lard or shortening until particles are the size of fine crumbs. Gradually stir in water until flour is moistened and dough almost cleans side of bowl.
2. Turn out on lightly floured board. Knead until smooth.
3. Divide into 12 pieces and roll each into a ball. Cover with plastic film and let rest for 20 minutes.
4. Flatten each ball into a 4 or 5 inch patty. Using a rolling pin, roll each patty from the center to the edges, making a thin 9-inch round. Turn dough often.
5. As each tortilla is shaped, place on preheated, dry, heavy griddle or heavy frying pan over medium heat, approximately 350ºF (175ºC).
6. Almost immediately little blisters will appear. Turn tortilla and press down gently but firmly with a broad spatula. When blisters form over most of the surface, turn over and repeat process, pressing until blisters are light brown. Tortilla should be soft. If tortilla sticks or browns too quickly, reduce heat.
6. Stack tortillas inside a folded cloth towel inside a plastic bag and let steam until all are cooked. May be served hot or wrapped in foil and stored in refrigerator.

Makes 12 tortillas.

Reheating Tortillas

Many recipes call for corn or flour tortillas to be softened or warmed before using. Here are some quick methods for warming tortillas: Place tortillas between moist microwavable paper towels (with tortillas separated by paper towels) and microwave for 20 to 45 seconds. Or place wrapped tortillas in a 250ºF (120ºC) oven for 15 minutes. Place inside plastic bag or tortilla warmer to keep soft.

Bread for the Three Kings

One of New Mexico's most festive foods and especially good eating.

1 package (¼ ounces) of active dry yeast
⅓ cup warm water 110ºF (45ºC)
1 cup of butter or margarine
¾ cup sugar
3 eggs
3 cups all-purpose flour
¾ cup golden raisins
¾ cup currants
4 tablespoons candied orange peel, chopped
4 tablespoons candied citron, chopped
4 tablespoons almonds, chopped
¼ teaspoon allspice
1 lima bean

1. Sprinkle yeast on the surface of the warm water and let sit for 10 minutes.
2. Preheat oven to 275ºF (135ºC).
3. Cream butter or margarine and sugar until fluffy. Beat in eggs one at a time. Add yeast water and beat thoroughly.
4. Coat raisins, currants, citron and orange peel with a little flour. Sift the rest of flour and spices into batter. Fold until blended. Add fruits and bean to mix.
5. Turn into a greased and floured ring mold. Bake for about 2 hours.
6. Remove from oven. Cool.

Makes 10 servings

This cake is served on El Dia de los Tres Reyes Magos, January 6. Place the cake on a serving plate and ring with a wreath of boxwood sprigs, similax, wandering Jew or juniper sprigs. Put a white candle, representing the Christ Child, in the center. Three additional candles—brown, yellow and black—are placed on the cake. The person who finds the bean in his or her slice is king or queen of the festivities and is especially blessed— and obligated to give another party on February 2 (also a religious holiday)!

Bread of the Dead

The Day of The Dead (November 2) is celebrated here with much merriment. This simple bread, which features the crossbones on its surface, is traditionally served in New Mexico on Halloween.

¼ cup milk
¼ cup butter, cut into small pieces
¼ cup plus 2 teaspoons of sugar
½ teaspoon salt
1 package (¼ ounces) of active dry yeast
¼ cup warm water 110ºF (45ºC)
2 eggs
3 cups all-purpose flour
¼ teaspoon cinnamon

1. In a small pan scald milk; remove from heat and stir in butter, ¼ cup of sugar and salt.
2. In a large mixer bowl, stir yeast into warm water and let stand until softened (about 5 minutes). Add milk mixture. Separate 1 egg; add yolk to yeast mixture (reserve white). Add remaining egg and 2½ cups of flour; beat until well blended.
3. Turn out on a well-floured board and knead until dough is smooth (about 10 minutes), adding more flour as needed. Place in a covered greased bowl; turn once to grease top. Cover with damp cheesecloth. Place in a warm place until dough has doubled (about 1½ hours). Punch dough down and knead briefly.
4. Cut off ½ cup of dough; wrap in plastic and set aside. Divide the remaining dough into 3 equal parts; shape each into a rope about 12 inches long. Braid ropes, pressing ends to hold securely. Place on greased baking sheet and join ends to make a small wreath. Divide reserved dough in half; shape each portion into a bone. Cross bones and place on wreath.
5. Cover lightly and allow to rise in a warm place until puffy (about 30 minutes). Gently beat reserved egg white and brush over bread. Mix cinnamon and remaining 2 teaspoons of sugar and sprinkle over bread, avoiding the bones. Bake in a preheated 350ºF (175ºC) oven until richly browned (about 35 minutes). Cut in wedges and serve warm.

Makes 8 to 10 slices.

Green Chile Cornbread Muffins

These are moist and do not crumble. The go well with all New Mexican meals. Try the different cornmeals for variety.

¾ cup milk
1 8-ounce can cream-style corn
⅓ cup melted butter or vegetable oil
2 eggs beaten
1½ cups white, yellow or blue cornmeal
1 teaspoon baking powder
½ teaspoon baking soda
1 teaspoon salt
1 teaspoon sugar
1½ cups mixed shredded cheddar cheese and Monterey Jack cheese
1 4-ounce can New Mexico green chiles, drained and chopped
    OR 3 to 5 fresh or frozen green chiles, roasted, peeled, seeded, deveined and chopped

1. Preheat oven to 400ºF (205ºC). Line 18 muffin cups with paper liners or grease and flour each cup.
2. In a medium-size bowl, stir together milk, corn, butter, and eggs.
3. In a large bowl, whisk together cornmeal, baking powder, baking soda, salt, and sugar. Add mixture from medium-size bowl to dry ingredients and mix just until combined. Do not over mix.
4. Spoon a large spoonful of batter into each prepared muffin cup, filling about ⅓ of each cup, and top with a little cheese mixture and green chile, dividing evenly and reserving a little for sprinkling on top. Top with remaining batter and reserved cheese and green chile. Each cup should be two-thirds full.
5. Bake 25 to 30 minutes, or until muffins are golden and a wooden pick inserted in the center comes out clean.

Makes 18 muffins.

Hopi Piki Bread

In a solemn ritual, with precise movements, Hopi Indians use blue corn meal to make Piki bread. One sheet of this paper-thin, delicate ceremonial bread is rolled into a scroll make one piki. It takes quite a bit of practice to get this one right.

¾ cup Hopi blue cornmeal
  OR commercial blue corn masa or cornmeal, finely ground or sifted
¾ teaspoon salt
4 cups water
1 teaspoon juniper ashes
¼ cup cornstarch mixed with 1 cup cold water
½ ounce sheep's brain
  OR 2 tablespoons vegetable shortening

1. In a 3-quart saucepan, combine cornmeal or masa and salt; slowly stir in water. Add the juniper ashes slowly, stirring with a wire whisk until mixture is smooth. When well mixed, bring to a boil, stirring constantly. Reduce heat, simmer 15 minutes, stirring occasionally.
2. Stir cornstarch and add to masa mixture. Bring to a boil and cook for 2 minutes, stirring constantly.
3. Heat an electric griddle to 350ºF (175ºC) or a cast-iron griddle over medium heat until a drop of water dances on the surface. Rub the griddle with sheep's brain or coat with shortening; when hot, add the batter ⅓ to ½ cup at a time. It works best to paint it onto the griddle with a pastry brush. Paint the center first, then the edges, forming a rectangle. Paint the edges twice. Take care the batter does not splatter on you. Bake until dry, about 4 to 5 minutes.
4. Carefully peel off the griddle and set aside.
5. Begin cooking second piki, following same directions. After it has begun to cook, place first piki on top and carefully fold over two opposite sides. Begin rolling from one of the sides not folded and carefully roll into a scroll. Set aside. Continuing with remaining batter until done.

Makes 6 to 8 pieces.

Piki bread is one of the Hopi traditional food items used in Hopi weddings, baby feasts and other significant dance days or kiva activities.

Note: Ashes may be purchased by mail order from Tsakurshovi, P. O. Box 234, Second Mesa, AZ 86043, phone (928) 734-2478. Tsakurshovi also carries traditional Hopi arts, crafts and cultural items, ceremonial items, and "Don't worry, be Hopi" t-shirts.

Pecan Biscuits

A bed-and-breakfast specialty, these biscuits are an excellent way to start your day. There is nothing like the smell of biscuits in the morning. The cinnamon and sugar make a nice topping.

1¾ cups all-purpose flour
3 tablespoons sugar
2 teaspoons baking powder
½ teaspoon salt
¼ cup shortening
1 egg beaten
¾ cup milk
⅓ cup pecans, finely chopped

Topping:
2 tablespoons sugar
½ teaspoon ground cinnamon

1. Preheat oven to 425ºF (220ºC).
2. In a medium-size mixing bowl, combine flour, sugar, baking powder and salt. Cut in shortening until mixture has appearance of coarse crumbs.
3. In a small bowl, combine beaten egg and milk; add all at once to dry mixture, stirring just until dough clings together. Stir in pecans.
4. Drop by heaping teaspoons onto a greased baking sheet.
5. For topping, combine sugar and cinnamon; sprinkle over biscuits.
6. Bake for 8 to 10 minutes.

Makes 36 biscuits.

Miniature Zucchini & Pecan Breads

Here is a fun recipe. Prepare this recipe as little breads served individually or as two large loaves. This bread also freezes beautifully.

1 cup all-purpose flour
2 cups stone-ground whole-wheat flour
1½ teaspoons baking powder
1 teaspoon baking soda
1 teaspoon salt
1 teaspoon ground cinnamon
½ teaspoon ground ginger
½ teaspoon ground nutmeg
½ teaspoon pumpkin pie spice
1 cup sugar
½ cup clover honey
2 large eggs
1¼ cups mayonnaise
¼ cup water
2 cups zucchini, grated unpeeled, packed
½ cup carrots, grated unpeeled, packed
1 teaspoon vanilla extract
¾ cup dark raisins
½ cup pecans or walnuts, chopped

Honey Cinnamon Butter:
½ cup soft butter
4 tablespoons honey
½ teaspoon cinnamon

1. Preheat oven to 350ºF (175ºC). Butter and flour 8 miniature loaf pans or two 3⅝ x 7⅜-inch loaf pans.
2. In a large bowl, mix together all-purpose flour, whole wheat flour, baking powder, baking soda, salt, cinnamon, ginger, nutmeg, pumpkin pie spice and sugar.
3. Add honey, eggs, mayonnaise and water. Beat well. Stir in zucchini, carrots, vanilla, raisins and pecans.
4. Pour batter evenly into 8 prepared miniature pans or divide evenly between 2 prepared 3⅝ x 7⅜-inch prepared loaf pans. Place pans on a cookie sheet and bake 35 minutes. Remove from oven and cool. Wrap each loaf in plastic wrap.

5. Prepare the Honey Cinnamon Butter. In a small bowl mix together butter, honey and cinnamon and blend until smooth. Serve with the breads.

Makes 8 miniature loaves or 2 regular-sized loaves.

Pecan & Cranberry Bran Muffins

I love muffins, so I am always on the outlook for unusual recipes. I found this one in a small cafe in Las Cruces. Enjoy its full rich flavor and texture.

1 cup oat bran
½ cup corn meal
⅔ cup all-purpose flour
2½ teaspoons baking powder
½ teaspoon salt
2 teaspoons non-fat dry milk powder
¼ cup pecans, chopped
¼ cup raisins
3 egg whites
2 teaspoons vegetable oil
¾ cup skim milk
⅓ cup honey
1 teaspoon vanilla extract
1 cup fresh cranberries, halved

1. Preheat oven to 400ºF (204ºC). Spray muffin pan with vegetable cooking spray or paper line muffin cups.
2. In a large bowl, combine bran, cornmeal, flour, baking powder, salt, dry milk powder, pecans and raisins; set aside.
3. In a medium bowl, beat egg whites with oil. Add skim milk, honey, vanilla and cranberries.
4. Combine dry and wet ingredients, stirring only to moisten. Batter will be lumpy. Spoon into prepared muffin pan. Bake 20 to 25 minutes or until wooden pick inserted into center comes out clean. Remove from pan; cool 5 minutes and serve.

Makes 12 muffins.

New Mexican Sweet Bread (Molletes)

Molletes are usually prepared for holidays. Worth the effort it takes to make them, these little breads will give you pleasing results.

Dough:
4 cups all purpose flour, sifted
1¼-ounce package active dry yeast
1 cup milk
¼ cup sugar
¼ cup shortening
1 teaspoon salt
2 medium eggs

Topping:
⅔ cup all-purpose flour
½ cup sugar
¼ cup margarine
2 egg yolks, beaten

1. Start with the dough. In a large bowl, combine the yeast and 2 cups of the flour.
2. In saucepan, combine milk, sugar, salt and shortening. Heat until warm and shortening begins to melt.
3. Pour into flour mixture. Add eggs and beat for ½ minute with electric mixer on low speed. Then beat at high speed for 3 more minutes.
4. By hand, stir in enough flour to make a stiff dough. Turn dough onto lightly floured surface and knead until smooth. Form into a ball and place into lightly oiled bowl. Cover and let rise until doubled.
5. While dough is rising, make topping. In a medium-size bowl, combine flour and sugar. Cut in margarine until mixture has appearance of fine crumbs. With a fork, slowly stir in eggs.
6. Dough should be soft. On a lightly floured surface, knead until smooth. Form 15 balls, roll each ball into a three inch circle; set aside.
7. Punch risen dough down and turn it out. Form into 15 smooth balls. On lightly floured surface, roll each ball into a 3-inch circle, about ½ inch high.

8. On a lightly greased cookie sheet, place dough circles about 2 inches apart. With spatula, place topping circles on top of dough circles. Slash tops with a crisscross pattern. Cover lightly and let rise until double.
9. Preheat oven to 375ºF (190ºC). Bake for 15 minutes.

Makes 15 molletes.

Peanut Honey Coffeecake

You must try this cake. It's quick and easy, but with a great taste. Of all my coffee cake recipes none is easier to make or better eating.

2 cups packaged biscuit mix
2 tablespoons sugar
1 egg, slightly beaten
⅔ cup milk
¼ cup honey
¼ cup creamy peanut butter

Topping:
½ cup packed brown sugar
½ cup packaged biscuit mix
¼ cup chopped peanuts
2 tablespoons butter
2 tablespoons creamy peanut butter
½ teaspoon ground cinnamon

1. Grease a 9 x 9 x 2-inch baking pan. Preheat oven to 400ºF (205ºC).
2. In a medium bowl combine biscuit mix and sugar. Add egg and milk. Blend in honey and peanut butter. The mixture will be lumpy.
3. Turn into prepared pan.
4. Combine topping ingredients until crumbly; sprinkle over batter. Bake for 20 to 25 minutes. Cool and cut into squares.

Makes 6 servings.

Potato Bread

Here is my Aunt Tiny's recipe for Potato Bread. It has great body and flavor and makes excellent sandwich bread.

1 cup warm whole milk
1 cup warm water
1½ packages (3½ teaspoons) active dry yeast
2 tablespoons honey
6 to 7 cups all-purpose flour
½ pound small red potatoes
1 tablespoon salt
3 tablespoons corn oil
1 egg plus 1 tablespoon milk or water, beaten, for egg wash

1. In a large bowl, combine the milk and water. Stir in the yeast and let it dissolve, then add the honey and 3 cups of the flour. Beat vigorously with a spoon to form a thick, smooth batter. Cover and let rise in a warm place until doubled in size, about 45 minutes.
2. While the dough is rising, boil or steam the potatoes, leaving the skins on if you like. In a second large bowl, mash the cooked potatoes with a fork and set them aside to cool. Once the dough has risen, add the potatoes, oil and salt. Mix well.
3. Fold in about 2 more cups flour, ½ cup at a time, turning the bowl a quarter of a turn between folds to approximate the action of kneading. When the dough becomes too thick to handle in this way, turn it out onto a floured surface, and begin kneading. Knead the dough until the surface is smooth and satiny, 5 to 8 minutes, adding only enough flour to keep it from sticking.
4. Place the dough in an oiled bowl, turning it over so the top is coated. Cover it and let it rise in a warm place until doubled in size, about 45 minutes. Punch it down, and let it rise again, 35 to 40 minutes.
5. Preheat oven to 350ºF (175ºC).
6. Shape the dough into two loaves and place them in oiled pans. Let them rise until doubled, about 25 minutes.
7. Prepare the egg wash by beating together 1 egg and 1 tablespoon milk or water. Brush the tops of the risen loaves with the egg wash. Bake loaves for 50 to 60 minutes, until golden brown on all sides. Remove the loaves from the oven and turn them out onto a rack to cool.

Makes 2 loaves.

Ranch Buttermilk Bran Muffins

Here is a stick-to-your-ribs version of muffins—a sure winner. Healthful and hearty, these freeze well but are best when served hot from the oven.

1 cup buttermilk
1½ cup whole bran cereal
½ cup sugar
⅓ cup shortening
1 egg
1½ cups all-purpose flour
2 teaspoons baking powder
½ teaspoon baking soda
½ teaspoon salt

1. Preheat oven to 400ºF (205ºC). Spray a muffin pan with vegetable cooking spray.
2. In a bowl, stir together buttermilk and bran; let stand until liquid is absorbed.
3. In another bowl, thoroughly cream sugar, shortening and egg. Combine remaining ingredients and buttermilk-bran mixture.
5. Spoon batter into prepared muffin pan. Bake 25 minutes or until a wooden pick inserted into center comes out clean. Remove from pan; cool 5 minutes and serve.

Makes 12 muffins.

Sourdough Blue-Cornmeal Bread

The flavor and texture of sourdough blends well with the natural earthy flavor of blue corn. Truly a match of the centuries.

Sourdough Starter:
1¼-ounce package active dry yeast
2½ cups warm 110ºF (45ºC) water
2 cups all-purpose flour
1 tablespoon sugar

Bread:
1¼-ounce package active dry yeast
1½ cups warm 110ºF (45ºC) water
6 cups all-purpose flour
1 cup sourdough starter, room temperature
¼ cup honey
3 tablespoons butter, softened
2 teaspoons salt
1½ cups blue cornmeal
½ teaspoon baking soda
Blue cornmeal

Sourdough Starter:
1. In a glass or plastic bowl, soften yeast in a ½ cup warm water. Stir in remaining warm water, flour and sugar. Beat until smooth. Allowing for starter to expand, cover and let stand at room temperature 3 to 5 days, stirring 2 to 3 times each day. Time required depends on the room temperature—the warmer the room the shorter the time needed for the starter to ferment. Cover and refrigerate.
2. To keep starter going: After removing some starter, stir in 3/4 cup water, ¾ cup all-purpose flour and 1 teaspoon sugar to remainder. Let stand at room temperature at least 1 day until bubbly. Cover and refrigerate for later use. If not used in 10 days, add 1 teaspoon of sugar. Repeat adding sugar every 10 days. Starter can also be frozen.

Sourdough Blue-Cornmeal Bread:
1. In a large mixer bowl, soften yeast in water. Blend 3 cups of flour, sourdough starter, honey, butter and salt into the yeast-water mixture. Beat 3 to 4 minutes. Combine blue cornmeal and soda and stir into flour-yeast mixture. Stir in enough remaining flour to make a moderately stiff dough.
2. Turn out on a lightly floured surface and knead until smooth (8 to 10 minutes). Shape into a ball.
3. Place in a greased bowl; turn once to coat. Cover; let rise in a warm place till double (1½ hours). Divide in half and place in two greased loaf pans sprinkled with blue cornmeal. Cover and let rise till double (45 to 60 minutes).
4. Preheat oven to 375°F (190°C). Bake for 35 to 40 minutes.

Makes 2 loaves.

Spiced Pumpkin Bread

Every year around Halloween time, my wife makes this bread, and I can hardly wait for it to cool. The second loaf keeps well for 6 weeks if you wrap it in foil and freeze it.

1 cup vegetable oil
2 cups sugar
3 large eggs
1 16-ounce can solid pack pumpkin
3 cups all purpose flour
1 teaspoon cinnamon
1 teaspoon nutmeg
1 teaspoon ground cloves
1 teaspoon baking soda
½ teaspoon salt
½ teaspoon baking powder
1 cup coarsely chopped pecans

1. Preheat oven to 350ºF (175ºC). Butter and flour two loaf pans.
2. In a large bowl, beat oil and sugar to blend. Mix in eggs and pumpkin.
3. In a second large bowl, sift together flour, cinnamon, nutmeg, cloves, baking soda, salt and baking powder. Stir into pumpkin mixture in two additions. Mix in pecans.
4. Divide batter equally between two prepared loaf pans. Bake until wooden pick inserted into center comes out clean, about one hour and 10 minutes. Transfer pans to wire rack and cool for 10 minutes. Turn out bread onto racks by cutting along edges to loosen. Cool completely.

Makes 2 loaves.

Sweet Saffron Rolls

Pungent and aromatic, a little saffron goes a long way. If you want something special, these rolls are for you. I use this recipe for bunuelos or bread fritters. For fritters, fry in oil until brown on both sides.

½ cup warm 110ºF (45ºC) water
1 tablespoon sugar
1¼-ounce package of active dry yeast
½ cup butter
⅛ teaspoon saffron threads
3 eggs
3 to 3½ cups all-purpose flour
½ teaspoon salt
⅓ cup sugar

Glaze:
1 egg yolk
1 teaspoon of water

1. In a cup, mix water with 1 tablespoon sugar and sprinkle the yeast over it. Set aside until the surface is frothy. Stir gently.
2. In a skillet, melt butter and drop in saffron. Remove skillet from heat and swirl mixture. Let butter cool to warm. Place in a mixing bowl and thoroughly beat in eggs.
3. In a large mixing bowl, combine flour, salt and sugar. Pour in eggs and saffron butter mixture. Stir vigorously until the dough forms a mass and becomes difficult to work. Turn out onto a heavily floured surface; knead dough until smooth and elastic. Cover and let rise in a warm place about 30 minutes, until doubled.
4. Punch down dough and turn onto a floured surface; knead lightly for a few seconds. Shape into 16 balls and place close together on an ungreased baking sheet. Cover with a cloth, place in a warm place and let rise for about 30 minutes.
5. Make glaze by combining egg yolk and water. Uncover rolls and carefully brush tops with the glaze. Do not let glaze touch baking sheet.
6. Preheat oven to 375ºF (190ºC). Bake 12 to 15 minutes. Check after 10 minutes. If rolls are browning too quickly, cover with foil or slip another baking sheet under the first and lower the heat to 325ºF (160ºC). Rolls are done when they sound hollow when tapped on undersides. Serve warm.

Makes 16 rolls

MAIN DISHES

Here are a number of main dishes that offer taste, texture and color—experience the variety of full rich flavors found in New Mexico's exciting foods. From **Tacos, Burritos** and **Enchiladas** to new versions of some of the old standards like **Chimichangas** and **Carne Asada**, you will find these worthy of preparing. In addition, I also have included some newer recipes that are becoming very popular, such as **Corn Chowder Con Queso** and **Green Chili Cheeseburgers**. Many of these will be enhanced when served with the red or the green sauces you will find in the "Sauces" chapter of this cookbook (pp. 167–79).

I have also included my wife **Millie's Brisket** and a treat called **Four Beans & a Pea Cassoulet**, a sure-fire meal in a crockpot. Prepared from readily available canned goods, here's one you quickly mix together and put in a crockpot, then leave for the day. When you come home, you have a wonderful meal fit for a king.

Light 'n' Fancy Tostado Cups give you a chance to show off. This delicacy can even make folks refer to you as a Chef, yet it is simple and easy to put together. I have also included couscous, in **Santa Fe Chicken & Couscous**. I have recently learned to use this pasta in a number of ways and find it to be healthy and versatile. This recipe offers a good way for you to become acquainted with this North African staple, which is catching on in New Mexico.

Baked Chimichangas

Here is a different method of preparing a dish that is traditionally fried.

1 pound lean ground beef
¼ cup onion, finely chopped
1 tablespoon red wine vinegar
1 teaspoon ground red chiles
¼ teaspoon ground cinnamon
⅛ teaspoon ground cloves
1 4-ounce can New Mexico green chiles, drained and chopped
    OR 3 to 5 fresh or frozen green chiles, roasted, peeled, seeded,
    deveined and chopped
1 medium tomato, chopped
8 10-inch flour tortillas
1 egg, beaten
2 tablespoons butter or margarine, softened
red or green chile sauce (see Sauces chapter, pp. 167–79.)

1. In 10-inch skillet, cook beef and onion, stirring occasionally until beef is browned; drain.
2. Stir in vinegar, ground red chiles, cinnamon, cloves, green chiles and tomato. Bring to boil, then reduce heat and simmer uncovered for 20 minutes.
3. Warm tortillas (See p. 66).
4. Preheat oven to 500ºF (260ºC). Spoon ⅛ of the beef mixture onto the center of each tortilla and brush edges with beaten egg mixture. Fold envelope style to seal. Brush each chimichanga with butter or margarine and place seam side down on a large ungreased baking sheet.
5. Bake uncovered for 8 to 10 minutes or until tortillas begin to brown and filling is hot.

Serve with your favorite red or green sauce.

Makes 8 servings.

Beef Burritos

To satisfy a hearty appetite, try this old favorite. Cooked chicken can be substituted for the beef. Vegetarians can omit the meat and use more beans; some add rice and even avocado.

2 cups **New Mexican Meat Filling** (See p. 105.)
2 cups or 1 15.5-ounce can refried beans
8 10-inch flour tortillas
2 cups shredded lettuce
¼ cup tomatoes, chopped
½ cup dairy sour cream
1 cup shredded cheddar cheese
red or green chile sauce (see Sauces chapter, pp. 167–79.), warmed, added to taste

1. In a small skillet, heat New Mexican Meat Filling.
2. Warm tortillas (See p. 66).
3. In a small saucepan, heat the beans.
4. Spoon ¼ cup of meat mix onto center of each tortilla. Spoon 2 tablespoons of beans onto beef mixture. Top with lettuce, tomatoes, sour cream and cheese and your favorite red or green sauce.
5. Fold filled tortillas envelope style. If desired, pour more sauce over the burritos.

Makes 8 burritos.

Note: This is only one recipe. Burritos can be made in a wide variety of ways. Fillings for burritos are only limited by your preferences and your imagination!

Beef Enchiladas

Enchiladas are a staple in New Mexican cooking. The basic ingredients are actually quite simple—tortillas, sauce, filling, topping and often a garnish. Preparation is easy. Just fry corn tortillas briefly in hot oil, then dip them in sauce. Next place the filling in the center of the tortilla. Fold, stack or roll them then bake them. The popularity of this dish has triggered an infinite variety of fillings, cheese enchiladas and chicken enchiladas being the most popular other versions. Today enchilada sauce is readily available at your local grocery store, so preparation is simple. Try some of my sauces (See pp. 167–79). Here I use my **Red Chile Sauce** (See p. 174). Try adjusting the filling quantities and rolling tortillas individually then baking. Rolled or folded they are great! They can also be made flat with ingredients layered on top of each other.

½ pound lean ground round
½ medium sized white onion, chopped
½ cup **Red Chile Sauce** (See p. 174.) or canned enchilada sauce
¾ cup (3 ounces) each shredded Jack and Longhorn cheese
6 corn tortillas
½ cup sour cream
pitted ripe olives
½ cup **Guacamole** (See p. 27 or use commercial.)
vegetable oil

1. In a 9-inch frying pan over medium-high heat, crumble and brown beef, adding oil if necessary. Add onion and cook until soft.
2. Add half of the Red Chile Sauce, cover and simmer for 10 minutes. Stir occasionally. Cool slightly and add half of both shredded cheeses.
3. Fry tortillas in vegetable oil and dip into remaining Red Sauce.
4. In an ungreased 9-inch frying pan, overlap two tortillas and let them extend across one side of rim. Spoon ⅓ of the meat mixture down the center of the tortillas and fold over the filling. Repeat for remaining tortillas, placing them side by side. They should cover the bottom. Pour the remaining sauce over the top and spread remaining cheese evenly on sauce.
5. Bake uncovered in a 350-degree oven for 30 minutes or until heated through. Serve with guacamole and sour cream and sprinkle with olives.

Makes three servings.

Beef Fajitas

Before fajitas became popular throughout the Southwest, skirt steak was a cheap cut scorned by all but the most dedicated beefeaters. Since then, however, the price of skirt steak has doubled and redoubled. Today there is probably no more typically New Mexican dish than Fajitas. The beef filling is placed in the center of the tortilla and topped with the cooked vegetables. One end of the tortilla is folded up about one inch over the filling, and the sides are folded over to form a hand-held food treat. Traditionally a variety of side dishes are offered.

Marinade:
⅓ cup fresh lime juice
¼ cup tequila
1 teaspoon crushed dried oregano leaves (preferably Mexican oregano)
2 large cloves garlic, puréed or crushed
1 teaspoon finely chopped fresh cilantro or coriander
2 teaspoons ground cumin
1 teaspoon freshly ground black pepper
1 teaspoon salt

Fajitas:
1½ pounds flank (skirt) steak
¼ cup vegetable oil
1 red bell pepper, stemmed, seeded and thinly sliced
1 green bell pepper, stemmed, seeded and thinly sliced
1 yellow bell pepper, stemmed, seeded and thinly sliced
1 large white onion, thinly sliced
1 tablespoon minced garlic
8 warmed flour tortillas
½ cup shredded cheese of choice
1 cup shredded lettuce
½ cup sour cream

1. In a mixing bowl, combine lime juice, tequila, oregano, pureed garlic, cilantro, ground cumin, ½ teaspoon black pepper, ½ teaspoon salt and mix well.
2. Pour marinade over meat in shallow glass, plastic or other non-reactive container. Refrigerate overnight or up to 24 hours.

3. When meat is marinated, set oven control to broil. Remove beef; pat it dry and place it on rack in broiler pan. Broil with top 3 inches from the heat until brown, about 4 minutes per side.

4. Remove meat from oven and let it rest for 5 or 10 minutes. Cut it across the grain and diagonally into finger-length strips. Cover and keep warm.

5. Meanwhile, in a large skillet, heat vegetable oil over medium-high heat. Add the peppers and onions and cook, stirring, until the onions are soft and slightly caramelized, 12 to 15 minutes. Add the garlic, remaining salt and black pepper and cook, stirring, until the garlic is fragrant and soft, 1 to 2 minutes. Remove from the heat.

6. Divide beef strips among warmed tortillas and top with the vegetables. Garnish with shredded cheese, sour cream and lettuce. Serve immediately.

Serves 8.

My recommended side dishes are **Guacamole** (See p. 27.), **Pico de Gallo** (See pp. 186–87.), **Refried Beans** (See p. 125.), **Simple Salsa** (See p. 190) and **Spanish Rice** (See p. 127.).

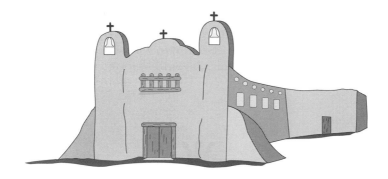

Beef Tacos

Tacos are the most popular American Mexican meal. In Spanish the word means simply "treat." A Taco is usually a crisp fried corn tortilla folded in half to form a pocket, filled with meat, a spicy sauce and a garnish. Commercially prepared Taco shells and Taco sauces are readily available a your local supermarket, making it easy to prepare them. In addition to prepared meat fillings, thin slices of leftover meat also work well. Tacos can be made with chicken or fish — and even with vegetable ingredients. Use your imagination. In this sample I use my **New Mexico Meat Filling** and **Hot Tomato Sauce**.

2 cups **New Mexico Meat Filling** (See p. 105.)
1 cup shredded sharp cheddar cheese
10 to 12 corn taco shells (purchased) or create your own. Heat ½ inch
    oil of choice in a wide frying pan over medium heat, 350ºF
    (175ºC). Fry corn tortillas one at a time until each becomes soft
    (about 10 seconds). Fold in half and hold slightly open with tongs
    so that there is a space between the halves for filling. Continue
    frying, turning as necessary, for about one minute until crisp and
    lightly browned.
½ cup **Hot Tomato Sauce** (See p. 169.)
2 large tomatoes, sliced thin or chopped coarse
2 to 3 cups of shredded Iceberg lettuce

1.   Heat the New Mexico Meat Filling and the Hot Tomato Sauce in medium and small saucepans. If using commercial taco shells, warm in the microwave.
2.   Place a heaping tablespoon of New Mexico Meat Filling in each taco shell pocket.
3.   Top Filling with tomatoes and shredded cheese.
4.   Dribble Hot Tomato Sauce on top of cheese. Top with shredded lettuce.

Serves 6.

Broiled Chicken with Tomato Raisin Sauce

A unique way to enjoy chicken—the tangy raisin sauce adds a new taste sensation.

3 tablespoons fresh cilantro, minced
6 garlic cloves, minced and divided
2 teaspoons freshly ground black pepper
1 pound skinless, boneless chicken, white or brown meat, cut into 1½-inch pieces
⅓ cup tomato sauce
1 tablespoon packed brown sugar
1 tablespoon cider vinegar
½ cup raisins

1. Preheat oven to 450ºF (230ºC).
2. In a small bowl, mix cilantro, 4 garlic cloves and black pepper. Rub mixture over chicken. Place chicken pieces well apart on lightly oiled 10 x 15-inch baking pan.
3. Bake or broil uncovered 20 to 25 minutes or until lightly browned and no longer pink in center.
4. In a food processor or blender, blend remaining 2 cloves garlic, tomato sauce, brown sugar, vinegar and raisins until raisins are chopped.
5. Serve chicken hot with tomato raisin sauce.

Makes 4 servings.

Burritos with Chile-Cheese Sauce

When I want to show off, I fix this delicious dish. The extra time it takes to prepare is worth the effort.

1 pound lean ground beef
½ cup chopped white onions
¼ teaspoon cumin
½ teaspoon dry-leaf oregano, crushed
1 teaspoon garlic salt
1 tablespoon cooking oil
1 15-ounce can pinto beans, drained
    OR 2 cups cooked pinto or black beans
    ½ cup cheddar cheese, grated
1 4-ounce can New Mexico green chiles, drained and chopped
    OR 3 to 5 fresh or frozen green chiles, roasted, peeled, seeded, deveined and chopped
6 white flour tortillas
salt to taste

Chile Cheese Sauce
1 can condensed cheddar cheese soup
1 4-ounce can chopped New Mexico green chiles, drained
    OR 3 to 5 fresh or frozen green chiles, roasted, peeled, seeded, deveined and chopped

1. Preheat oven to 350°F (175°C).
2. Brown beef in 10-inch skillet; drain off fat.
3. Add onions and sauté until translucent.
4. Add cumin, oregano and garlic salt.
5. In a small skillet, heat oil and add beans.
6. Mash beans with a potato masher and sprinkle with half the cheddar cheese.
7. Cover and cook over low heat until cheese is melted; add salt to taste.
8. Soften tortillas if necessary (See p. 66). Divide beans evenly among six tortillas; top each with evenly divide meat mixture. Spoon green chile over meat and top with remaining cheddar cheese.
9. Roll up each tortilla and place, seam-side down, on a greased cookie sheet.

10. Prepare the Chile Cheese Sauce. Heat cheddar cheese soup in a small saucepan over medium heat. Add chopped chiles and mix well.
11. Pour sauce over rolled burritos and heat in oven for 15–20 minutes.
12. Serve immediately.

Serves 3 to 6

Carne Asada (Grilled Steak)

Lime juice and spices enhance the steak, and grilling adds the final touch.

¼ cup olive oil
6 garlic cloves
2 tablespoons lime juice
2 teaspoons dried-leaf rosemary
½ teaspoon ground red New Mexico chile
½ teaspoon dried-leaf oregano
¼ teaspoon ground cumin
2 pounds beef flank steak
3 medium white onions, cut into ½-inch slices
warmed and softened flour or corn tortillas (See p. 66.)
Red or green sauce (See pp. 167–79.)
Guacamole (See p. 27.)

1. In a blender or food processor, puree olive oil, garlic, lime juice, rosemary, ground chile, oregano and cumin.
2. Rub garlic-herb paste on both sides of steaks.
3. Broil steaks 4 inches from heat source for 6 to 8 minutes per side.
4. In small skillet heat oil and cook onions until soft.
   OR grill steaks and onion slices over medium coals until meat is medium rare, 12 to 15 minutes. Turn once. Onions should be tender in 15 to 18 minutes.
5. Thinly slice steak across grain. Serve wrapped in warm tortillas with red or green sauce and guacamole.

Makes 4 to 6 servings.

Chalupas

Hot and spicy—great company fare—this festive traditional dish is a fine example of the full rich taste of New Mexican cooking.

2 pounds lean pork, cubed
4 tablespoons vegetable oil, divided
2 tablespoons all-purpose flour
1 cup water
1 teaspoon ground cumin
garlic salt to taste
1 14-ounce can 14 ounces tomatoes, chopped
4 4-ounce cans New Mexico green chiles, drained and chopped
    OR 12 to 20 fresh or frozen green chiles, roasted, peeled, seeded, deveined and chopped
8 corn tortillas, fried crisply
2 whole boneless chicken breasts
2 7-ounce cans chicken broth
3 cups **Refried Beans** (See p. 125.)
2 cups **Guacamole** (See p. 27.)
1½ cups (6-ounces) grated cheddar cheese
1 cup (8 ounces) dairy sour cream
red or green sauce (See pp. 167–79.)

1. In a 10-inch skillet, heat 3 tablespoons vegetable oil and fry corn tortillas one at a time until crisp. Drain on paper towels and set aside.
2. In large Dutch oven or heavy pot, heat 1 tablespoon vegetable oil; brown pork. Stir in flour, then add water, cumin, garlic salt, tomatoes and green chiles. Simmer until thick, stirring occasionally.
3. In saucepan, simmer chicken breasts in chicken broth 15 minutes. Remove from broth and shred. Set aside.
4   To assemble, begin with tortilla; top with layer of heated refried beans, pork in sauce, shredded chicken, guacamole, cheese and sour cream.

Serve with your favorite red or green sauce.

Makes 8 servings.

Chicken Burritos with Black Beans & Papaya

Papaya gives these burritos a sweetness that, when combined with the heat of the chile, presents the ultimate in sassy taste.

4 chicken breast halves, boned and skinned
1 14.5-ounce can chicken broth
1 bay leaf
½ teaspoon ground cumin
½ cup white onion, chopped
1 tablespoon oil of choice
1 16-ounce can black beans, drained and rinsed
2 jalapeño peppers, seeded and finely chopped
8 10-inch flour tortillas
1 ripe papaya, seeded, peeled and thinly sliced
1 cup shredded Monterey Jack cheese
¼ cup fresh cilantro, snipped
your favorite red or green sauce (See pp. 167–79.)

1. In a skillet, place chicken breasts, chicken broth, bay leaf and cumin. Bring to boil. Reduce heat, cover and simmer, turning as necessary, for 15 to 20 minutes or until chicken is tender and no longer pink. Remove bay leaf.
2. Drain and reserve ¼ cup of broth. Let chicken stand until cool.
3. Heat oil in large skillet. Cook onion until soft but not brown. Add beans, jalapeño peppers and reserved ¼ cup of broth.
4. Preheat oven to 350F° (175°C). Mash bean mixture. Meanwhile, stack tortillas and wrap tightly in foil. Heat in preheated oven 2 minutes to soften.
5. Spread about 3 tablespoons bean mixture down the middle of each tortilla.
6. Using a fork, pull chicken into long thin threads.
7. Top each tortilla with shredded chicken, papaya slices, shredded cheese and cilantro.
8. Fold filled tortillas envelope style and secure with toothpick.
9. Place burritos on a baking sheet. Cover loosely with foil. Place in 350°F (175°C) oven and bake until heated thoroughly.
10. Heat red or green sauce and serve with burritos.

Makes 4 to 6 servings.

Chicken Tamale Pie

Mildly spiced chicken and vegetables are hidden under a blanket of cornmeal.

3 tablespoons paprika
2 tablespoons white vinegar
3 garlic cloves, minced
1½ teaspoons dried-leaf oregano
½ teaspoon ground cumin
2 cups low-sodium chicken broth
2 large white onions, minced
2 tablespoons fresh mint minced,
    OR 1 teaspoon of dried mint
⅛ teaspoon anise seeds
3 cups bite-sized pieces cooked chicken
2 large ripe tomatoes, cut into wedges
2 tablespoons cornstarch
fresh cilantro for garnish (optional)
your favorite red or green sauce (See pp. 167–79.)

Topping:
½ cup masa harina or cornmeal
½ cup all-purpose flour
1½ teaspoons baking powder
1 large egg white
1½ teaspoons vegetable oil
½ cup non-fat milk

1. Preheat oven to 400ºF (205ºC). In a 2-quart saucepan, combine paprika, vinegar, garlic, oregano, ground cumin and minced onions with ½ cup chicken broth. Blend into a smooth paste. Add remaining broth, mint and anise seeds. Bring to a boil, then reduce heat and simmer for 5 minutes, stirring frequently.
4. Dissolve cornstarch in water and set aside. In a deep 3-quart baking dish, combine broth mixture, chicken pieces, tomatoes and cornstarch mixture, making an even layer.
5. Make Topping. In a small bowl combine masa harina, flour, baking powder, egg white, oil and milk. Spread evenly over filling.
6. Bake about 50 minutes until filling is bubbly in center and topping is browned. Remove and let stand for 5 minutes. Serve with red or green sauce and garnish with cilantro sprigs.

Makes 6 servings.

Corn Chowder Con Queso

Enjoy a hearty meal in one dish. I serve this with sourdough bread and a simple green salad.

1 tablespoon butter or oil
2 medium white onions, chopped
¾ cup celery, chopped
3 cups frozen whole kernel corn, thawed
1 large unpeeled potato, finely chopped
1 red bell pepper, chopped
1 can (14.5 ounces) low-salt chicken broth
1 14.5 ounce can diced tomatoes
2 jalapeño chiles, seeded and finely chopped
1 tablespoon chile powder
½ teaspoon salt
¼ teaspoon ground cumin
1 cup skim milk
2 tablespoons cornstarch
2 tablespoons chopped fresh cilantro
4 ounces shredded Monterey Jack cheese

1. In a large Dutch oven or heavy pot, heat butter or oil to sizzling and add onions and celery. Cook until soft.
2. Stir in corn, potato, bell pepper, broth, tomatoes, jalapeño peppers, chile powder, salt and ground cumin. Over medium heat, bring to a full boil then reduce heat. Cover and cook 15 to 18 minutes until potatoes are fork tender.
3. In a small bowl, stir 2 tablespoons of milk into cornstarch until smooth. Stir in remaining milk then stir mixture into soup. Cook 3 to 4 minutes over medium high heat until mixture comes to a full boil.
4. Reduce heat to low. Cook, stirring occasionally, 5 minutes. Stir in cilantro. Serve topped with cheese.

Makes 8 servings.

De Baca Lamb Stew

The Emillio De Baca family shared this dish with me, and it is a wonderful way to fix lamb. A special dish from a special family.

¼ cup oil
1 medium white onion, diced
3 garlic cloves, minced
½ teaspoon New Mexico red chile, ground
½ teaspoon ground cumin
¼ teaspoon salt
¼ teaspoon black pepper, ground fine
1 pound boneless leg of lamb, fat removed, cut into ½-inch cubes
6 medium red potatoes, cut into ½-inch cubes
½ cup carrots, peeled and diced
½ cup frozen green peas
¼ cup fresh cilantro, chopped
2 cups chicken stock
4 cups cooked white rice

1. In a large Dutch oven or heavy pot, heat oil then add onion, garlic, ground red pepper, cumin, salt and black pepper. Cook until onions are soft.
2. Add lamb and sauté for 3 to 4 minutes or until lightly browned.
3. Add remaining ingredients. Bring to a boil, reduce heat and simmer for 30 to 35 minutes or until potatoes are tender.
4. Serve over warm cooked rice.

Makes 4 servings.

Four Beans & a Pea Cassoulet

Get out your crockpot and let this simmer. When you return from work or play you will have a delightful supper ready. Chickpeas are called garbanzo beans in Latin America.

1 16-ounce can stewed tomatoes, undrained and cut up
1 15.5-ounce can butter beans, drained
1 15.5-ounce can great northern beans, drained
1 15.5-ounce can black beans, drained
1 15.5-ounce can kidney beans, drained
1 15.5 ounce can garbanzo beans (chickpeas), drained
1 cup carrots, finely chopped
1 cup white onions, chopped
2 garlic cloves, chopped
3 to 5 fresh or frozen green chiles, roasted, peeled, seeded, deveined and
    finely chopped
    OR 1 4-ounce can New Mexico green chiles, drained and chopped
2 teaspoons dried parsley flakes
1 teaspoon dried basil leaves
½ teaspoon dried thyme leaves
½ teaspoon salt
⅛ teaspoon fresh ground black pepper
1 bay leaf

1. In a 2-quart slow cooker, combine all ingredients. Cover and cook on high setting for 30 minutes. Reduce to low setting; cook for 5 to 6 hours or until vegetables are tender. Remove bay leaf before serving.

Makes 8 servings.

Green Chile Cheeseburgers

I love to use water-soaked hickory chips for grilling. You may broil the hamburgers if you prefer or if you don't have access to a grill. This is a New Mexico version of an old favorite with a spicy yellow-orange mayonnaise that is colorful and sassy.

2 cups hickory chips (if grilling)
3 tablespoons low-fat or nonfat plain yogurt
1 4-ounce can New Mexico green chiles, drained and chopped
    OR 3 to 5 fresh or frozen green chiles, roasted, peeled, seeded,
    deveined and chopped
⅓ cup green onions, finely chopped
¼ teaspoon dry sage, crushed
½ teaspoon salt
½ teaspoon black pepper, freshly ground
2 pounds lean ground beef
6 ounces Monterey Jack cheese, cut into 8 slices
8 Kaiser rolls, split and toasted
leaf lettuce
sliced tomato

Saffron Mayonnaise:
1 egg yolk, room temperature
2 cloves garlic, roughly chopped
½ teaspoon salt, preferably coarse sea salt
½ cup olive or peanut oil
½ teaspoon cayenne pepper
½ teaspoon saffron threads, dissolved in 1 teaspoon hot water
lemon juice, to taste

1. At least one hour before grilling, soak hickory chips (if using) in enough water to cover.
2. In a large mixing bowl, combine yogurt, green chilies, onions, sage, salt and pepper. Add ground beef and mix well. Shape into eight ¾-inch-thick patties.
3. To grill, arrange medium-hot coals around a drip pan in a covered grill. Test for medium heat above pan. Drain hickory chips and place on top of coals. Place burgers on grill rack over the drip pan

but not over the coals. Lower the grill hood. Grill burgers until no longer pink, turning once.
4. To broil, place burgers on the unheated rack of a broiler pan. Broil 3 inches from the heat for 15 to 18 minutes or until burgers are no longer pink, turning once.
5. Top each patty with cheese the last 2 minutes of grilling or broiling time.
Serve patties on rolls with lettuce, tomato and Saffron Mayonnaise.

Saffron Mayonnaise:
1. If the egg is cold from refrigerator, set in bowl of hot water for 1 minute or so to warm it up.
2. Pound the garlic with the salt in a mortar. The coarse grains of the sea salt work especially well for breaking down the garlic until it forms a smooth paste. Add the egg yolk, and stir briskly for about a minute with the pestle.
3. Whisk in the olive oil or peanut oil as for a mayonnaise, drop by drop at first, then adding it in larger amounts as you go along. When all the oil is incorporated, add the cayenne and the dissolved saffron. Season to taste with lemon juice.

Makes 8 servings.

Grilled Lamb Patties

Sheep ranching is a major livestock activity in New Mexico. Lamb is regularly served with many of our family meals.

1 pound ground lamb
1 tablespoon canola oil
6 tablespoons piñon nuts
¼ teaspoon ground coriander
⅛ teaspoon ground cumin
1 teaspoon chile powder
salt to taste
⅓ cup ice water

1. Place meat in a medium-size bowl.
2. In a small skillet, heat oil; sauté nuts in oil until they are lightly golden and drain on paper towels.
3. Mix nuts, coriander, cumin and chile powder with meat. Add salt to taste.
4. Add ice water, a little at a time. Mix until incorporated.
5. Shape into 4 patties; refrigerate 2 hours before grilling.
6. Grill patties, 5 minutes per side.

Makes 4 servings.

Indian Corn Casserole

Here is a wonderful old way to prepare corn that is as good today as it was 25 years ago when I first made it. Even today, as soon as my garden corn grows tall, I can't wait to get fresh corn and fix it once again.

4 ears fresh corn, with husks
3 cups zucchini, grated
1 cup white onion, minced
1 4-ounce can New Mexico green chiles, drained and chopped
    OR 3 to 5 fresh or frozen green chiles, roasted, peeled, seeded,
    deveined and chopped
½ cup all-purpose flour
1 teaspoon ground cumin
1 teaspoon ground chili powder
¼ teaspoon salt
½ teaspoon freshly ground black pepper
¼ teaspoon New Mexico red chile powder
2 15.5-ounce cans black beans, drained
    OR 4 cups cooked dried black beans

1. Husk corn, reserving 12 husks; rinse husks thoroughly.
2. In a large saucepan, bring 1 quart of water to a boil; add husks and remove from heat. Cover and let stand for 15 minutes. Drain and pat dry with paper towels. Line 2-quart baking dish with softened husks, allowing excess to extend over sides.
3. Preheat oven to 325ºF (160ºC).
4. Cut whole kernels from 2 ears of corn; set aside. Grate corn from remaining ears, pressing firmly to remove pulp. Add grated corn to cut corn; set aside.
5. In a large non-stick skillet, combine zucchini, onion and chiles. Cover and cook over medium-low heat 10 minutes, stirring occasionally. Add flour, cumin, chili powder, salt, ground black pepper and ground red chile; stir well. Add corn and beans; stir. Cook, uncovered, 4 minutes, stirring frequently.
6. Spoon mixture into prepared dish. Fold extended ends of husks toward center, overlapping. Bake for 25 minutes.

Makes 6 servings.

Light 'n' Fancy Tostado Cups

Once in a while, everyone likes to show off, and this is one of my best. If you want to impress that special friend or guest, this is worth the effort.

1 pound beef flank or round steak, partially frozen
6 7-inch flour tortillas
1 cup salsa (See pp. 180–194 or use commercial.)
1 teaspoon cornstarch
1 medium zucchini, cut into julienne strips, about 2 cups
4 green onions, sliced
1 tablespoon oil
½ cup Monterey Jack cheese, shredded
cherry peppers for garnish (optional)
lettuce leaves

1. Preheat oven to 350ºF (175ºC).
2. Slice beef across grain into bite-sized strips. An electric knife may be helpful in slicing the beef. Set aside.
3. For tostada cups, spray a 6-cup muffin tin with non-stick cooking spray. Brush tortillas lightly with warm water or soften in microwave (See p. 66). Starting at the outer edge of each tortilla and going toward the center, cut six 4-inch long slits in spoke-like fashion. Gently press tortilla into muffin tin, overlapping edges to form cups. Bake for 12 to 15 minutes or until crisp. Remove from cups and set aside.
4. Combine salsa and cornstarch and set aside.
5. Spray a large skillet with vegetable spray and preheat. Add onions and cook only until soft, then add zucchini and cook and stir over high heat 1½ minutes. Remove vegetables from skillet.
6. Add oil to skillet and cook beef slices, ½ at a time, 2 to 3 minutes or until done. Return all beef to skillet. Reduce heat and stir in sauce. Cook and stir until thickened and bubbly, then cook an additional 2 minutes longer.
7. Stir in vegetables. Place each tostada cup on lettuce-lined serving plates. Spoon in meat mixture and top with cheese. Garnish with cherry peppers (optional).

Makes 6 servings.

Millie's Brisket

No one fixes better brisket than my wife, Millie. The secret is a tight seal that retains the moisture. This should be prepared a day ahead.

2 beef bouillon cubes
2 cups hot water
¼ cup light sodium-reduced soy sauce
3 tablespoons Liquid Smoke
1 4–5 pound beef brisket
garlic powder to taste

1. In saucepan, dissolve bouillon cubes in hot water. Add soy sauce and Liquid Smoke. Set aside.
2. Place brisket in Dutch oven. Sprinkle with garlic powder. Pour bouillon mixture over brisket and cover with foil, place lid over foil, making a tight seal.
3. In a preheated 300ºF (150ºC) oven, bake for 6 hours. Refrigerate, then before serving time, slice across the grain and place meat back in roaster or serving casserole with all of the liquid. Reheat (about 1 hour) and serve.

Makes 8 servings.

Mushroom & Pepper Quesadillas

Quesadillas can be made with many combinations of different ingredients. Have fun creating your own combinations.

2 tablespoons oil
1 white onion, finely chopped
1 pound fresh mushrooms, sliced
1 garlic clove, minced
1 tablespoon fresh oregano, minced
1 10.5-ounce can tomato soup
8 10-inch flour tortillas
2 red bell peppers, seeded and finely sliced
2 or 3 fresh or frozen green chiles, roasted, peeled, seeded, deveined and finely chopped
    OR 1 4-ounce can New Mexico green chiles, drained and finely chopped
2 cups Monterey Jack cheese, grated
sour cream
your favorite red or green sauce (See pp. 167–79.)

1. Preheat oven to 350ºF (175ºC).
2. In large skillet, heat oil; add onion, mushrooms, garlic and oregano. Stir frequently and cook until onion is soft.
3. Stir in tomato soup and heat thoroughly.
4. Place 4 tortillas on a lightly greased baking sheet and spoon tomato mixture onto them. Top with bell peppers, chiles and cheese. Top with another tortilla.
5. Bake for 10 minutes or until cheese is melted.
6. Cut into quarters and serve immediately with sour cream and red or green sauce.

Makes 4 servings.

New Mexico Meat Filling

This spicy meat filling freezes well and will save you valuable time in the preparation of the numerous recipes. Use it as a filling for burritos, tamales, tostados and flautas. A must in a New Mexico kitchen.

5 pounds beef roast
3 tablespoons oil
2 white onions, chopped
1 4-ounce can New Mexico green chiles, drained and chopped
    OR 3 to 5 fresh or frozen green chiles, roasted, peeled, seeded,
    deveined and chopped
2 7-ounce cans green chile salsa
¼ teaspoon garlic powder
4 tablespoons all-purpose flour
salt to taste
2 teaspoons ground cumin
juices from roast

1. Preheat oven to 350ºF (175ºC). Place roast in 4 to 6-quart baking dish, cover and roast 2½ hours or until well done. Drain the meat, reserving juices. Cool and remove fat and bones. Shred meat and set aside.
2. In a large skillet, heat oil; add onions and green chiles. Sauté for 1 minute. Stir in salsa, garlic powder, flour, salt and cumin. Cook for 1 minute longer. Stir in reserved meat juices and shredded meat. Cook for 5 minutes or until thickened. Can be used at once or packed into freezer containers.

Makes about 9 cups.

Posole

My first taste of this dish was in Taos, and this is the same recipe. I have prepared it many times, and although I have since found many more versions, this one is still special to me.

1 pork loin roast, about 3 pounds
5 cups water
2 cups onion, chopped
2 teaspoons salt
1 whole chicken, about 2½ pounds
3 cups chicken broth
1½ tablespoons bacon grease
2 garlic cloves, crushed
1½ tablespoons chili powder
½ teaspoon paprika
2 16-ounce cans white hominy, drained

Garnishes:
chopped white onions
sliced radishes
sliced avocado wedges

1. In a large Dutch oven, place pork roast and water. Bring to a boil. Add onions and salt. Reduce heat, cover and simmer gently for 30 minutes. Add chicken and chicken broth and bring to a boil again. Reduce heat, cover and simmer for 45 minutes. Remove pork and chicken from broth and allow to cool. Cover and refrigerate broth to help congeal fat. Remove fat from surface when cooled.
2. Cut pork and chicken meat into small pieces and discard bones.
3. In skillet, heat bacon grease. Add garlic, chili powder and paprika; stir just until blended. Add small amount of cooled broth and stir. In a large saucepan, add chili mixture and hominy to rest of broth and bring to a boil. Reduce heat, cover and simmer gently for 30 minutes. Add pork and chicken pieces, and simmer until meat is thoroughly heated, about 15 minutes.

Serve in individual bowls with garnishes as side dishes.

Makes 8 servings.

Quick Mini-Tamales

Tamale-making is an old art form. I think you have to be born into the tradition of tamale-making. Here is a quick substitute that makes a wonderful appetizer or side dish.

2 cups masa flour (masa harina)
¼ cups chicken broth
¼ teaspoon salt
½ cup vegetable oil
2 cups **New Mexico Meat Filling** (See p. 105.)
your favorite red or green sauce (See pp. 167–79.)

1. Cut 30 pieces of aluminum foil, each 6-inches square.
2. In a mixing bowl, combine masa flour, chicken broth, salt and oil. Mixture will be thick. Spread about ½ tablespoon of masa mix in a 3-inch square in the center of each piece of foil. Spoon about ½ tablespoon of meat mix down the center of each masa square.
3. Fold foil edges together so masa covers filling. Seal all sides by folding.
4. Place a steamer rack in a large pot. Pour in boiling water to a depth of 1 inch. Stack tamales on rack. Arrange so that steam can circulate freely. Do not allow tamales to touch water. Bring water to boil, cover and maintain boiling. Cook, adding boiling water as needed to keep water level at 1 inch. Cook about 1 hour until masa is firm. Remove from foil and serve hot with red or green sauce.

Makes 30 small tamales.

Note: If corn husks are available, the process is basically the same. Soften the corn husks by soaking. Pat masa into each husk, then spread the center with several spoonfuls of above filling. Fold masa-lined husk around filling to make a little packet. Stack packets in a steamer and steam until masa dough is cooked and firm.

Santa Fe Chicken & Couscous

This is an excellent example of a new direction that is adding a unique element to the ever-changing cuisine of New Mexico.

½ teaspoon ground cumin
⅛ teaspoon fresh ground black pepper
1 pound chicken breast halves, boneless and skinless
1½ cups water
2 teaspoons chicken bouillon granules
dash fresh ground black pepper
1 cup uncooked couscous
1 cup whole-kernel corn, drained
¾ cup tomato, chopped and seeded
¼ cup green onion, sliced

1. Spray 10-inch skillet with non-stick cooking spray.
2. In small dish, mix ¼ teaspoon of the cumin and ⅛ teaspoon black pepper; sprinkle over both sides of chicken breast halves. Add chicken to skillet, cook for about 9 minutes or until brown on both sides.
3. Add ½ cup water, bouillon granules, the other ¼ teaspoon of the cumin and a dash of black pepper. Bring to boil then reduce heat. Cover and simmer 7 minutes or until chicken juices run clear.
4. Remove chicken from skillet. Stir in remaining cup of water and bring to a boil. Stir in couscous, corn, tomato and onion; place chicken breast pieces on top. Remove from heat; cover and let stand for at least 5 minutes until all water is absorbed.

Makes 4 servings.

Couscous is a pre-cooked granular form of semolina. It is a versatile staple of North Africa that is gaining popularity here. Used like rice, it may also be served with milk as porridge, with a dressing as a salad or sweetened and mixed with fruits for dessert.

Spanish Chicken Skillet Supper

This is another recipe that features pecans. I am constantly amazed at the many uses for this popular nut. I hope you give this one a try. I recommend it highly.

2 tablespoons butter
½ cup pecans, coarsely chopped
1 cup instant rice, long grain
1 garlic clove, minced
1 14.5-ounce can stewed tomatoes
1 14-ounce can chicken broth
1 teaspoon chili powder
½ teaspoon ground cumin
½ teaspoon salt
1 cup cooked chicken, diced
2 small zucchinis halved lengthwise, cut into ½-inch slices
½ cup green onions, sliced with tops
1 4-ounce can New Mexico green chiles, drained and chopped
    OR 3 to 5 fresh or frozen green chiles, roasted, peeled, seeded,
    deveined and chopped
½ cup Monterey Jack cheese, shredded
2 tablespoons fresh cilantro, chopped

1. In large skillet, heat butter. Add pecans; cook until lightly toasted. Remove, drain on paper towels and set aside.
2. Add rice and garlic to skillet; cook and stir for 1 minute. Add tomatoes, chicken broth, chili powder, cumin and salt. Bring to boil; reduce heat. Cover tightly and simmer 15 minutes.
3. Add chicken pieces, zucchini, onions and green chile; cover and continue to simmer 5 minutes. Remove from heat; let stand covered for 5 minutes or until liquid is absorbed. Sprinkle with shredded cheese, reserved pecans and cilantro.

Makes 4 servings.

Stuffed Mexican Cabbage

A good example of the cultural blending that produces some of New Mexico's unusual fare, this is a contribution from the Germanic community in Albuquerque.

1 medium head cabbage
½ pound pork sausage
1 pound ground beef
1 onion, grated
1½ cups green chiles, roasted, peeled, seeded and chopped
½ teaspoon garlic salt
1½ cups apples, thinly sliced and peeled
1 onion, chopped
1 16-ounce can sauerkraut, rinsed and drained
1 cup chicken broth
1 cup tomato juice

1. Core cabbage. Place in a large pot and cover with water. Heat to boiling then reduce heat and simmer for 5 minutes. Remove cabbage from water and cool. Pull leaves off one at a time; you should have about 10 large leaves. Trim away vein ends of leaves.
2. In a skillet, combine sausage and ground beef, and cook 15 to 20 minutes. Add grated onion and cook until onion is clear. Drain off excess fat. Add green chiles and garlic salt; mix well. Cool.
3. Using ⅓ cup of meat and chile mixture, spread some near the vein of each leaf. Fold the end over the stuffing, then fold over the sides, envelope-fashion, and roll as tightly as possible.
4. Preheat oven to 350ºF (175ºC). In a bowl, mix apples, chopped onion and sauerkraut. Spread half of this mixture on the bottom of deep baking dish or casserole. Place cabbage rolls on sauerkraut. Spread remaining mixture on top.
5. Mix broth and tomato juice, pour over rolls. Cover and place in oven. Bake 1 hour.

Makes 4 to 5 servings

Wilma's Chicken 'n' Chile Casserole

Here is a casserole dish that is sure to please. I first tasted this dish when I stayed as a guest in Santa Fe after an art show.

2 cups cubed cooked chicken
1 10¾-ounce can condensed cream of mushroom soup.
1 10¾-ounce can condensed cream of chicken soup
1 cup chicken broth
1 4-ounce can New Mexico green chiles, drained and chopped
    OR 3 to 5 fresh or frozen green chiles, roasted, peeled, seeded, deveined and chopped
1 cup sour cream
1 cup white onions, chopped
1 4-ounce can sliced mushrooms
1 9-ounce bag corn tortillas chips
1 cup grated cheese

1. Preheat oven to 350°F (175°C).
2. Mix together soups, broth, mushrooms, sour cream, chiles and chicken.
3. Layer bottom of a 9 x 12-inch casserole with ½ of the corn chips.
4. Add ½ of chicken soup mixture, onions and cheese.
5. Repeat layer of chips, then add remaining mixture, remaining onions and balance of cheese on top.
6. Bake for 30 minutes.

Serves 6.

VEGETABLES & SIDE DISHES

Like many other ethnic-based cuisines, New Mexico's food is going through a period of change. The rich cultural transition that New Mexico is currently experiencing is starting to have an effect on our food. For centuries, New Mexican cuisine has been based on Native American and Spanish influences. With Anglos, Asians and African-Americans having an ever-increasing percentage of the population, new foods are appearing regularly. Nowhere is it more noticeable than in new vegetables and side dishes. The arrival of many imported vegetables and new fruits as well as a trend toward healthier eating have contributed to many new dishes.

In spite of these changes, I still prefer the old faithful vegetable grouping of corn, squash and pinto beans. In this book I present a number of unusual combinations of traditional staples that feature corn, beans and squash. I think you will like them. These versions of old traditional dishes will add spice, color, texture and nutrition to your meals.

Preparing Dried Beans

A Southwestern staple, dried beans keep almost indefinitely. Before cooking, rinse beans well and sort through them, tossing out any small stones or other matter. Some beans require soaking prior to cooking, which can be done on the stove top, in a crockpot or in a pressure cooker. Cooking times vary depending on the kind of bean. Properly prepared, cooked beans are tender but still firm. When you are short of time or only need a small amount of beans, you will find canned varieties useful, although they are sometimes mushy.

There are many schools of thought when it comes to cooking beans. Some soak the beans overnight; others say there is no need to soak them at all. Because hard water can affect cooking times, if you have that in your home, you should use distilled or drinking water when cooking beans. With all methods, for 2 cups of beans, add 2 tablespoons of bacon grease, lard or vegetable shortening (to cut down on foaming and help prevent boil-over) and 2 cloves of garlic (optional). Do not add vinegar, tomatoes or other acidic ingredients; they will hinder cooking. You can add them when the cooking is essentially completed. You may, however, add onion, herbs and spices as flavoring while cooking the beans. Choose whatever method suits you best from the following three options:

If you do not plan to soak, wash 2 cups of beans, remove debris, broken or bad beans, and add 8 cups of water. Remove any beans that float to the top. Bring to a full boil in a large kettle and simmer for 3 or 4 hours, adding boiling water as needed. Keep water level slightly higher than the top of the beans. Continue cooking until the beans are tender. Add 2 teaspoons of salt before serving.

Soaking the beans overnight softens them for cooking and helps reduce their gas-producing properties. For soaking the beans, wash 2 cups of beans and remove any debris, broken or bad beans. Cover with 6 cups of cold water and remove any beans that float to the top. Let them sit overnight. Drain and rinse well. You can also quick soak them: place 2 cups of beans in 6 to 8 cups of water and heat to a boil. Boil for 3 minutes, then remove from heat and let them sit for 2 to 4 hours. Drain and rinse well.

After soaking beans, place rinsed beans in a large kettle with bacon grease, lard or shortening and enough water to cover the beans. Bring to a boil and cover. Simmer for 1½ to 2 hours or until tender, adding hot

water as needed to keep the beans covered. If you use a crockpot, heat on high for 2 to 3 hours then on low 6 to 8 hours or until done.

I prefer to use a pressure cooker. When pressure cooking, I use 2 cups of washed and sorted beans and place them with 5 cups of distilled water in a pressure cooker. Next I add one tablespoon of vegetable oil per cup of beans to reduce frothing. I bring the water to a gentle boil for about 10 minutes. Then I remove them from the heat, put the lid on the cooker and let them sit for at least 2 hours. One hour before I intend to eat, I drain and rinse the beans, then add enough distilled water to cover and 2 teaspoons of salt. I cover the beans and bring the cooker up to 15 pounds of pressure for 12 minutes. This time may need to be adjusted longer for higher altitudes. Then I remove the cooker from the stove and allow the pressure to drop naturally.

Whichever method you use, you will enjoy having fresh beans to serve as a side dish or as an ingredient in other recipes. Cooked beans will keep up to four days in the refrigerator and can be frozen.

Anasazi Beans with Chiles & Tomatoes

Try these speckled beauties—revived ancient heirloom beans, related to pinto beans but much sweeter. Their mottled burgundy/white markings fade when cooked. They hold their shape and cook faster than pinto beans.

2 cups dry Anasazi beans
6 cups distilled water
2 tablespoons vegetable oil
½ small white onion, chopped
1 garlic clove, chopped
1 14.5-ounce can tomatoes, undrained and chopped
½ cup vegetable broth
¼ teaspoon ground cumin
1 4-ounce can New Mexico green chiles, drained and chopped
    OR 3 to 5 fresh or frozen green chiles, roasted, peeled, seeded, deveined and chopped
salt and pepper to taste

1. Prepare beans using one of the methods above. They will cook more quickly than pinto beans—about 2 hours or until beans are soft. Drain and cool.

2. Heat oil in heavy skillet. Add onions and garlic and cook until soft. Add tomatoes with liquid, vegetable broth and cumin. Bring to a boil and reduce heat. Cover and simmer 5 minutes, stirring occasionally.
3. Add beans and chiles to mixture and cook on low 10 minutes. Season with salt and pepper to taste.

Makes 4 to 6 servings.

"Anasazi" is a term often used to denote the modern Pueblo Indians' ancestors who lived in the Four Corners country of southern Utah, southwestern Colorado, northeastern Arizona and northwestern New Mexico from about AD 200 to 1300. They are known to have mastered stonemasonry, surface mining, water control systems, road engineering and pottery. The meaning of the Navajo word "Anasazi" was thought to be "ancient ones" but actually is "ancient enemies." As such, the term has lately fallen out of favor, being replaced by "Ancestral Pueblo."

Fiesta Corn

Quick and easy, this is a side dish you will serve again and again.

2 cups fresh or frozen corn kernels
¼ cup water
¼ cup New Mexico green chiles, roasted, peeled, deveined, seeded and chopped
2 tablespoons green olives, chopped
2 green onions, diced

1. Cook corn in water for 6 to 8 minutes over medium heat.
2. Drain and add chiles, green olives and onions.
3. Stir and cook briefly until thoroughly warmed.

Makes 4 servings.

Baked Beans New Mexico Style

These are certainly not Boston baked beans but have a special flavor all their own. As a rule I always cook dry beans in distilled water; try it and see if you notice the difference.

1 pound dried pinto beans
6 cups distilled or drinking water
2 tablespoons chicken-flavored bouillon granules
1 12-ounce bottle dark beer
1 medium onion, chopped
6 cloves garlic, minced
3 jalapeño peppers, seeded and minced
¼ cup **Three Chile Sauce** (See p. 178.)
3 tablespoons brown sugar, packed firm
3 tablespoons vinegar
1½ tablespoons Worcestershire sauce
½ teaspoon ground cinnamon
Red Chile Sauce (See p. 174.)

1. Rinse beans, remove debris and floating or broken beans then cover with at least 1 inch of water. Let them sit overnight. Drain and rinse well. Set aside.
2. In an 8-quart Dutch oven, combine 6 cups distilled water, bouillon granules, dark beer, onions and garlic. Add reserved beans. Bring to a boil. Lower heat, cover and cook beans gently for 2 hours or until soft, stirring occasionally.
3. Stir in jalapeno peppers; simmer, uncovered, for 30 minutes.
4. Place beans in a 2-quart baking dish. Add Three Chile Sauce, brown sugar, vinegar, Worcestershire sauce and cinnamon. Bake uncovered in a preheated 350ºF (175ºC) for 30 minutes.
5. Top with Red Chile Sauce and serve.

Makes 6 to 8 servings.

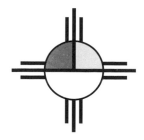

Baked NuMex Big Jim Chiles Rellenos
with Corn Stuffing

I love chile rellenos, but the fried version has too high a fat content for some people. Here's a new way to enjoy them. If you are trying to cut back on fat, try these.

2 tablespoons butter
1 medium white onion, chopped
1 garlic clove, minced
3 cups fresh or frozen whole-kernel corn, thawed
1 large ripe red tomato, peeled and chopped
¼ teaspoon salt
⅛ teaspoon fresh ground black pepper
⅛ teaspoon ground oregano
3 cups Monterey jack cheese, shredded
12 NuMex Big Jim New Mexico chiles, roasted, peeled, seeded and
    deveined (if not available try fresh poblano or Anaheim chiles)
Red Chile Sauce (See p. 174.)

1. After roasting and peeling, prepare chiles by making a small slit in each chile to remove the seeds and veins.
2. Preheat oven to 350ºF (175ºC) and grease a large shallow baking dish.
3. In large skillet, heat butter. Add onions and garlic and cook until onions are soft. Add corn, tomato, salt, pepper and oregano and simmer, uncovered, 15 to 20 minutes. Remove from heat. Stir in 2 cups of shredded cheese and cool.
4. Stuff chiles with corn mixture and place in a prepared baking dish. Sprinkle with remaining cheese. Bake uncovered 25 minutes or until sauce is bubbly and cheese is lightly browned.
5. Spoon Red Chile Sauce down the center of the chiles and serve.

Makes 4 to 6 servings.

Chiles Rellenos

Each year I wait for the new crop of green chiles to become available, and the first dish I prepare is Chiles Rellenos. I know of no better way to enjoy fresh green chiles. You can also use this batter for many other deep-fried vegetables or shrimp tempura.

8 large New Mexico green chiles with stems attached, roasted and
    peeled
½ pound longhorn, cheddar or Monterey Jack cheese
3 cups oil for frying
1 cup all-purpose flour
½ teaspoon salt
½ teaspoon sugar
pinch baking soda
1 egg
½ teaspoon of oil
1 cup ice water
Red or Green Sauce of choice (See pp. 167–79.)

1. Make a small slit on the side of each chile pepper to remove seeds and veins. Leave stems on chiles. Cut cheese into strips the length of each chile; they should be about 1 inch wide and 1/4 inch thick. Carefully insert a piece of cheese into each chile. Pat dry and refrigerate for at least 30 minutes.
2. Heat 3 cups oil in deep skillet or deep fryer to 375ºF (190ºC).
3. In a medium sized bowl, combine flour, salt, sugar, and baking soda. In a small bowl, beat egg, oil and cold water together with a fork. Combine with flour mixture. Do not overmix. Use at once.
4. Dip chilled chiles one at a time into batter. Allow excess batter to drip off. Slide coated chile gently into hot oil. Fry until golden brown on both sides. Drain on paper towel.
5. Serve immediately with red or green sauce.

Makes 4 servings.

Chile Soufflé

This soufflé can be easily prepared for two meals by splitting into four small casserole dishes. Simply double the recipe and freeze two unbaked soufflés; at a later date, thaw them and bake as directed.

3 tablespoons butter
3 tablespoons all purpose flour
1 cup whole milk
3 egg yolks
½ cup cottage cheese
½ cup tomatoes chopped and drained
2 tablespoons green onions, chopped
1 4-ounce can New Mexico green chiles, drained and chopped
    OR 3 to 5 fresh or frozen green chiles, roasted, peeled, seeded,
    deveined and chopped
salt
fresh ground black pepper
4 egg whites

1. Preheat oven 350ºF (175ºC).
2. In a saucepan, melt butter and stir in flour. Using a whisk, blend in milk. Over medium heat, cover and cook until thick. Remove from heat and whisk in egg yolks one at a time. Fold in cottage cheese, tomatoes, onions and chiles. Salt and pepper to taste.
3. In medium bowl, beat egg whites until they form stiff peaks. Thoroughly fold about ½ of egg whites into yolk mixture. Add remaining whites and fold in quickly, leaving some streaks of the whites showing.
4. Pour mixture into one-quart soufflé dish. To make the center rise higher than the edges, run a finger around inner rim of the dish to make a trough in the egg mixture. Bake 30–35 minutes, until deep golden brown.

Makes 4 servings.

Fried Green Tomatoes with Chile

Corn meal and chiles give an unexpected taste to this adaptation of an old Southern dish that is sure to please.

¾ cup finely ground cornmeal
½ teaspoon salt
1¼ pounds green tomatoes
2 tablespoons butter
4 fresh or frozen New Mexico green chiles, roasted, peeled, seeded, deveined and chopped
    OR 1 4-ounce can New Mexico green chiles, drained and chopped

1. In a shallow bowl, combine cornmeal and salt.
2. Cut tomatoes into ½-inch strips. Dip each slice in cornmeal, making sure it is completely covered.
3. In heavy skillet, melt butter. Over medium heat cook tomato slices until brown on both sides. Spread chiles evenly over the tomato slices, cover and steam 5 minutes or until chiles are hot.

Makes 4 to 6 servings.

The tomato, native to South America, became popular in the US in the 1900s. The green tomato has a piquant flavor that makes it excellent for frying, broiling or adding to salsas. Dozens of varieties are available today—differing widely in size and shape. The tomato most commonly used in New Mexican cooking is the beefsteak tomato, which is delicious both raw and cooked.

Fried Squash Flowers

The blossoms of either summer or winter squash are edible and delicious. They are very perishable and should be refrigerated for no longer than a day before using.

1 cup parmesan cheese, grated
1 cup ricotta cheese, crumbled
2 red bell peppers, roasted, peeled, seeded and diced
2 ounces sun-dried tomatoes, reconstituted and diced
2 tablespoons fresh basil, chopped
12 large squash flowers, tightly closed
2 eggs
2 tablespoons water
½ cup all-purpose flour
salt and fresh ground black pepper to taste
½ cup peanut oil

1. In a medium bowl combine ½ cup of the parmesan cheese with the ricotta cheese, bell peppers, reconstituted tomatoes and basil. Mix thoroughly.
2. Gently open flowers and stuff each with the cheese mixture, closing flower around the stuffing.
3. In a small bowl whisk the eggs with water.
4. In another small bowl, combine remaining Parmesan cheese and flour with salt and pepper to taste.
5. Dip flowers in egg mixture, then coat with flour and cheese mixture.
6. In a large skillet or Dutch oven, heat oil. Sauté flowers about 1 minute, or until golden brown. Drain on paper towels.

Makes 4 servings.

Green Beans in Jalapeño Dressing

I like green beans fixed this attractive way. The zest of the lime and the fire of the jalapeño pepper add new life to fresh green beans.

1½ pounds fresh green beans
1 cup water
2 medium oranges, cut into wedges

Dressing:
1 egg yolk
¼ cup lime juice
1 jalapeño chile, seeded and chopped
2 tablespoons olive oil
1 tablespoon sugar
1 tablespoon prepared mustard
2 teaspoons grated lime rind
¼ teaspoon fresh ground black pepper

1. Rinse and trim beans; cut into lengths to fit the width of food processor food chute. Position slicer disk in food processor; stack beans on their sides in the food chute. Using gentle pressure, push and slice beans. Repeat until all beans are sliced.
2. Place beans and water in 3-quart saucepan. Bring to boil. Cover and reduce heat; simmer 2 minutes or until beans are tender. Drain beans and arrange on serving platter.
3. Make dressing. Place egg yolk, lime juice, jalapeno pepper, olive oil, sugar, mustard, lime peel and pepper in food processor bowl. Process until blended.
4. Arrange orange wedges around the beans and top with dressing. Serve immediately.

Makes 6 servings.

Grilled Spanish-Style Eggplant

Try to choose the youngest eggplants you can find. As the plant matures, the skin becomes tough and the eggplant tends to be bitter.

2 small eggplants
1 tablespoon coarse salt
2 tablespoons garlic cloves, chopped
2 jalapeño chiles, seeded and finely minced
1 teaspoon red chile powder
½ cup light soy sauce
¼ cup toasted sesame oil

1. Slice eggplants lengthwise into ⅛-inch thick pieces. Sprinkle with coarse salt and set aside for 20 minutes. Pat with paper towel to remove excess moisture. This helps eliminate some of the acid taste.
2. In a large bowl combine garlic, jalapeño chile peppers, chili powder, soy sauce and toasted sesame oil. Whisk together. Add eggplant slices and marinate 4 to 6 hours.
3. Heat a large non-stick skillet. Cook slices for 3 or 4 minutes on each side until lightly browned.

Makes 4 servings.

The eggplant is a member of the nightshade family and is related to the tomato and potato. Though commonly thought of as a vegetable, it is actually a fruit. It's a good source of folic acid and potassium. Its sponge-like structure causes it to absorb fat or oil.

Indian Corn Pudding

I first tasted this pudding many years ago in Albuquerque. It is one you acquire a taste for and once hooked, you will want it again and again.

3 tablespoons butter or margarine
1 small white onion, chopped
½ garlic clove, minced
1 medium green bell pepper, seeded and chopped
¼ cup all-purpose flour
½ teaspoon salt
1 teaspoon sugar
⅛ teaspoon fresh ground black pepper
1 16-ounce can cream-style corn
3 eggs, lightly beaten
1 cup milk

1. Preheat oven to 350ºF (175ºC). Butter a 2-quart dish and set aside.
2. In saucepan, heat butter or margarine; add onion, garlic and bell pepper. Cook, stirring often, 5 minutes until onion is soft. Stir in flour, salt, sugar and pepper; cook, stirring, until thickened.
3. Remove from heat. Add corn, eggs and milk, stirring until mixture is well blended.
4. Pour mixture into prepared baking dish. Bake uncovered about 55 minutes until center is set. Test by gently shaking dish.

Makes 4 servings.

Refried Beans

Refried beans are an important ingredient in many New Mexican meals. Here is a way to enjoy them with lowered fat content.

4 ounces coarsely chopped bacon
2 chopped, white onions
2 garlic cloves, minced
4 cups cooked pinto or black beans
    OR 2 15.5-ounce cans of pinto or black beans, reserving liquid
½ cup low-sodium chicken broth
    OR reserved liquid from canned beans
2 tablespoons white vinegar (or to taste)
fresh ground black pepper to taste

1. In a large non-stick skillet, fry bacon about 4 minutes, stirring frequently until it begins to brown. Drain and return 1 tablespoon of drippings to skillet.
2. Add onions and garlic and cook 6 or 7 minutes until onions are soft. Break up bacon into bits and return to skillet.
3. To the skillet, add beans and chicken broth or ½ cup of the reserved liquid from the beans. Coarsely mash beans; season to taste with vinegar and black pepper.

Makes 6 servings.

Although the pinto bean is king in New Mexico, many other beans are a part of today's delicious taste treats. Among the most popular are Lima, black, Anasazi, red kidney, and garbanzo or chickpea.

Sassy Stuffed Tomatoes

Colorful and excellent eating, this is the kind of dish that will give you a reputation for being a great cook.

4 medium firm tomatoes
½ cup dairy sour cream
3 tablespoons jalapeño chile, seeded and chopped
3 tablespoons green bell peppers, seeded and chopped
3 tablespoons green onions, sliced
2 tablespoons all-purpose flour
¾ teaspoon sugar
½ teaspoon salt
1 ounce Monterey Jack cheese, shredded
¼ cup Cheddar cheese, shredded
jalapeño chile slices for garnish

1. Cut ¼-inch slice from the stem end of each tomato. If necessary, cut a thin slice off the other end so that tomatoes will sit upright. Using a teaspoon, gently remove the seeds and juice of each tomato. Place tomatoes upside down on paper towels to drain.
2. In a small bowl, combine sour cream, peppers, onions, flour, sugar and salt; mix well.
3. Place tomatoes upright on a foil-lined broiler pan or baking sheet. Spoon sour cream mixture into tomatoes. Broil 3 to 5 inches from heat for 2 to 3 minutes or until sour cream is bubbly and lightly browned. Sprinkle tomatoes with cheeses; broil 2 to 3 minutes longer until cheese is melted. Garnish with jalapeño chiles, if desired.

Makes 4 servings.

Spanish Rice

The perfect accompaniment for beef, chicken or seafood.

4 tablespoons vegetable oil
2 tablespoons butter
2 cups long grain rice
1 large white onion, chopped
2 garlic cloves, minced
3 to 5 fresh or frozen New Mexico green chiles, roasted, peeled, seeded,
    deveined and chopped
    OR 1 4-ounce can New Mexico green chiles, drained and chopped
⅛ teaspoon dry leaf oregano
¾ pound tomatoes, peeled, seeded, and chopped
¼ cup tomato puree
4 cups chicken broth
fresh ground black pepper to taste
¼ cup fresh cilantro, chopped

1. In a large saucepan, heat butter and oil. When butter is melted, add
   rice. Stirring constantly, cook 3 to 4 minutes until lightly browned.
2. Add onion, garlic, chiles and oregano; cook for additional 5
   minutes, stirring frequently.
3. Add tomatoes, tomato puree and chicken broth and bring to a boil.
   Reduce heat, cover and simmer about 20 minutes until liquid is
   absorbed and rice is tender. Remove from heat and stir in cilantro.

Makes 6 servings.

Spicy Garbanzo Beans & Vegetables

From Roman times, the garbanzo bean (or chickpea) has been an important food. Here it is—all dressed up in a New Mexico dish, served over rice.

1 tablespoon olive oil
½ cup sliced white onion
2 garlic cloves, finely chopped
2 cups sliced carrots
4 cups sliced zucchini
1 15.5-ounce can garbanzo beans, undrained
1 4-ounce can New Mexico green chiles, drained and chopped
    OR 3 to 5 fresh or frozen green chiles, roasted, peeled, seeded,
    deveined and chopped
1 teaspoon chicken bouillon granules
½ teaspoon salt
2 cups hot cooked rice
1 teaspoon fresh cilantro, minced

1. Heat oil in a 3-quart saucepan. Add onion and garlic and cook until soft.
2. Stir in remaining ingredients except rice and cilantro. Bring to boil, stirring occasionally; reduce heat. Cover and simmer for 12 to 14 minutes or until vegetables are crisp-tender. Serve over hot rice. Garnish with cilantro.

Makes 4 servings.

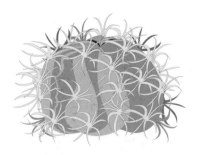

Squash & Tomato Con Queso

Con queso means "with cheese" in Spanish. The tart flavor of chevre (goat) cheese is the secret of this dish. It delivers an unexpected taste.

4 cups water
4 medium yellow crookneck squashes
2 large ripe tomatoes
¼ cup fresh dillweed, minced
2 tablespoons fresh basil leaves, minced
2 Hungarian yellow wax peppers seeded and sliced into rings
1 cup (8 ounces) chevre (goat) cheese, crumbled

1. Preheat oven to 400°F (205°C)
2. Heat water in a 2-quart saucepan. Add squash and bring to a boil. Reduce heat; simmer 2 to 3 minutes until tender.
3. Remove from heat; drain immediately. Rinse with cold water. Cut into ¼-inch slices. Set aside.
3. Trim both ends from tomatoes and discard. Cut tomatoes in half crosswise to form 2 thick slices each; set aside.
4. Cut four 12-inch pieces of heavy-duty foil. Place 1 tomato slice on each piece. Place squash slices on tomatoes. Sprinkle with dillweed and basil. Top with pepper rings and chevre cheese.
5. Fold to seal packets, place on baking sheet. Bake for 15 to 20 minutes.
Serve immediately.

Makes 4 servings.

Chevre cheese is pure white goat cheese. It has a delightfully tart flavor that easily distinguishes it from other cheeses. Ranging in texture from moist and creamy to dry and semi-firm, chevre cheese comes in a variety of shapes and takes on a sour taste when it is old. After opening, always wrap it tightly and store in refrigerator.

Wild Rice

¼ cup butter
½ pound fresh mushrooms, sliced
1 garlic clove, minced
1 tablespoon red bell pepper, seeded and minced
1 teaspoon jalapeño chile, seeded and minced
1 cup wild rice, rinsed and drained
½ cup slivered almonds
1 teaspoon salt
fresh ground black pepper
3 cups chicken broth

1. Preheat oven to 375ºF (190ºC).
2. In a large skillet, heat butter. Add mushrooms, garlic, bell pepper, jalapeño pepper, wild rice, almonds, salt and pepper. Stir-fry 2 minutes.
3. Add broth, stir until mixed. Spoon into a large shallow baking dish. Cover tightly. Bake about 1 hour or until rice is tender and liquid is absorbed.

Makes 6 servings.

Wild rice is known for its nutty flavor and chewy texture. Not really rice but the seed of a marsh grass native to the northern Great Lakes area, it has been harvested by Indians in Canada and the U.S. for centuries. It is important to clean wild rice carefully before using. Although it takes an hour to cook, be careful not to overcook it, as it will become starchy. Wild rice is especially nice as a side dish for all wild game.

CHILI

Any New Mexico cookbook can be considered incomplete without chili recipes. Chile-mania is becoming an obsession to more people each year, and in the U.S. some people even consider chili cooking a national pastime. Thousands of dollars in prize money provide incentives for real competition at local and regional cookoffs. I no longer compete but still enjoy visiting and judging these events. The cooks are a warm, fun-loving group, and I especially appreciate the recipes I have received from "Chiliheads" since the publication of my first two cookbooks.

This chapter presents chili dishes from the classic to the unusual, starting with the original **Bowl of Red**. Included are chicken and turkey dishes along with some new variations on old themes. Also included is a **Competition Chili** that has taken first place in several chili cookoffs.

With all the attention chili is getting, I hope that the relatively simple **Bowl of Red** will not get lost in the shuffle. It is, and always will be, real chili to me.

I should add a reminder that the word "chili" here refers to dishes containing chile peppers as well as other ingredients such as beans and meats. The word "chile" refers only to the type of pepper.

Bowl of Red

Here is my favorite, the dish that may have started the chili-mania.

2 tablespoons vegetable oil
1 large white onion, coarsely chopped
3 garlic cloves, finely chopped
3 pounds lean beef, coarse grind
4 tablespoons ground hot New Mexico red chile
4 tablespoons ground mild New Mexico red chile
2 teaspoons ground cumin
1½ teaspoons salt
3 cups water

1. In a 4-quart Dutch oven or heavy pot, heat oil. Add onion and garlic; cook until soft.
2. Add beef, ground chiles and cumin. Cook until meat is evenly browned, breaking any lumps with fork.
3. Add salt and water. Bring to a boil then reduce heat. Simmer uncovered 2 to 3 hours, stirring occasionally, until meat is very tender and flavors are fully blended. Add more water as necessary.

Serves 6.

The exact origin of chili is still debated today, but some New Mexicans claim it was started by a chuckwagon cook who ran out of black pepper. Looking for a substitute, he tried the little red peppers commonly used by the local Indians and Mexicans, and thus "Bowl of Red" was born. Purists say, "If you want chili, make chili; if you want beans, cook beans." In New Mexico we have no such prejudices—some even say that chili tastes better with beans.

Brisket Chili

This delicious chili made from brisket needs to be cooked slowly. I add beans for extra fullness and flavor.

vegetable cooking spray
2 pounds lean brisket, cut into ½-inch cubes
2 cups white onion, chopped
1 cup green bell pepper, seeded and chopped
3 fresh serrano chile peppers, seeded and finely chopped
3 cloves garlic, minced
2 tablespoons chili powder
1 teaspoon ground cumin
½ teaspoon dried-leaf oregano
¼ teaspoon ground New Mexico red chile
⅓ cup masa harina or cornmeal
1 14.5-ounce can whole tomatoes, undrained and chopped
1 13.5-ounce can beef broth
1 12-ounce can beer
2 tablespoons white vinegar
salt to taste

1. Coat a large Dutch oven with cooking spray; heat until hot. Add brisket and cook 5 minutes, stirring frequently, until meat is browned. Drain well and set aside. Wipe drippings from Dutch oven with a paper towel.
2. Re-coat Dutch oven with cooking spray. Add onion, bell pepper, serrano pepper and garlic; sauté 5 minutes or until soft.
3. Return brisket to Dutch oven. Add chili powder, cumin, oregano and ground red chile; stir well. Sprinkle mixture with masa harina; stir well. Add tomatoes, beef broth and beer.
4. Bring to a boil then reduce heat and simmer, partially covered, 1½ hours. Add vinegar and continue to simmer, partially covered, 30 minutes or until meat is tender.

Makes 8 servings.

Chicken & Rice Chili

One of the most unusual chili recipes, surprisingly good, very good! It is also very low in fat and calories.

1 tablespoon oil of choice
1½ pounds chicken thighs, skinned, boned, meat cut into ½-inch
    pieces.
1 medium white onion, chopped
½ cup long grain rice, uncooked
2 16-ounce cans stewed tomatoes
1 14.5 ounce can low-salt chicken broth
1¼ cups water
1 15.5-ounce can pinto beans, drained and rinsed
1 tablespoon chili powder
⅛ teaspoon salt
⅛ teaspoon ground black pepper

1. In 4-quart Dutch oven or heavy pot, heat oil. Over medium high heat, cook chicken 5 to 8 minutes or until browned, stirring frequently.
2. Add onion; cook 3 to 5 minutes or until onion is soft. Add remaining ingredients. Bring to a boil and reduce heat to medium; cover and cook 25 to 40 minutes or until rice is tender and chicken is no longer pink.

Makes 5 to 6 servings.

Chili Verde

This traditional recipe is one of my oldest and best.

1 pound lean boneless pork shoulder
1 28-ounce can tomatoes, undrained
2 medium white onions, chopped
1½ cups celery thinly sliced
1 teaspoon dried-leaf oregano
½ teaspoon powdered sage
2 bay leaves
1 large green bell pepper, seeded and chopped
3 New Mexico green chiles, roasted, peeled, seeded and chopped
    OR 1 4-ounce can New Mexico green chiles, drained and chopped
4 cups cooked white rice
salt
fresh ground black pepper
cilantro for garnish

1. Trim all fat from pork and cut into ¾-inch cubes.
2. In a large Dutch oven or heavy pot, add pork and ⅓ of the liquid
   from the tomatoes. Bring to rolling boil; reduce heat and simmer
   covered for 30 minutes.
3. Uncover pot; add onions, celery, oregano and sage. Cook over high
   heat, stirring frequently, until liquid has evaporated and pan
   drippings are browned (8 to 10 minutes). Add bay leaves.
4. Stir in tomatoes and their remaining liquid, breaking tomatoes up
   with a spoon. Reduce heat, cover and simmer for 30 minutes. Stir in
   bell peppers and chiles; cover again and continue to simmer,
   stirring occasionally, until meat is very tender. Continue to simmer
   uncovered until mixture is as thick as you like.
5. Remove bay leaves. Spoon over rice and garnish with sprigs of
   cilantro.

Makes 4 servings.

Chorizo Chili

Chorizo may be new for you. Be adventurous and try this highly-seasoned Mexican sausage the next time you make chili.

2 tablespoons oil
2 small white onions, chopped
½ pound chorizo sausage, slightly frozen
2 small green bell peppers, seeded and chopped
3 garlic cloves, minced
3 15-ounce cans whole tomatoes, undrained and cut up
3 8-ounce cans tomato sauce
2 10.5-ounce cans condensed beef broth
1 12-ounce can beer
2 4-ounce cans New Mexico green chiles, drained and chopped
    OR 6 to 10 fresh or frozen green chiles, roasted, peeled, seeded,
    deveined and chopped
2 tablespoons ground red chile powder
½ tablespoon ground cumin
1 teaspoon cayenne pepper
½ teaspoon dried-leaf oregano
½ teaspoon cinnamon
3 15.5-ounce cans of kidney beans, drained and rinsed
6 tablespoons cheddar cheese, shredded

1. In a large Dutch oven or heavy pot, heat oil. Add onions and sausage. Cook until onions are soft and drain.
2. Add remaining ingredients except kidney beans and cheese; bring to boil. Reduce heat and simmer uncovered for 1½ to 2 hours, stirring occasionally.
3. Add kidney beans; simmer until thoroughly heated. Garnish as desired with cheese.

Makes 10 to 12 servings.

Competition Chili

If you would like to enter a chili cookoff, this recipe is a proven winner.

2 teaspoons vegetable oil
3 pounds sirloin tip roast, course ground or cut into small pieces
1 white onion, chopped
1 14.5-ounce can beef broth
1/2 teaspoon dried-leaf oregano
3½ tablespoons ground cumin, divided
6 cloves garlic, chopped, divided
1 teaspoon mild New Mexico ground chile powder, divided
5 teaspoons hot New Mexico ground chile powder, divided
1 8-ounce can tomato sauce
1 14.5-ounce can chicken broth
1 teaspoon Tabasco pepper sauce
1 teaspoon brown sugar
1 tablespoon lime juice
salt to taste

1. In a large Dutch oven or heavy pot, heat oil. Cook meat until lightly browned.
2. Add onion and enough beef broth to cover meat. Bring to boil and cook for 15 minutes. Add oregano and ½ of the cumin, ½ of the garlic and ½ of both chile powders. Reduce heat to medium and cook for 10 minutes.
3. Add tomato sauce, remaining garlic, remaining beef broth and enough chicken broth for desired consistency. Cook for one hour over medium heat, stirring occasionally.
4. Add remaining chile powders and rest of the cumin. Simmer 25 minutes, stirring occasionally.
5. Add Tabasco sauce, brown sugar, lime juice and salt to taste. Simmer to desired consistency.

Makes 8 servings.

Easy Chipotle Chili

The sweet smoky flavor of the chipotle chile imparts an unusual taste. I have learned to like the chipotle and also use it in mole sauces.

4 dried chipotle chiles
2 teaspoons vegetable oil
½ medium white onion, coarsely chopped
2 garlic cloves, minced
1 pound lean beef, coarsely ground
¼ teaspoon dried-leaf oregano
¼ teaspoon ground cumin
2 10-ounce cans tomato soup
1 10.5-ounce can onion soup
2 16-ounce cans kidney beans, drained

1. Cover chiles with warm water. Let stand for 1 hour until softened. Drain and finely chop.
2. In a 4-quart Dutch oven or heavy pot, heat oil. Add onion and garlic; cook until soft.
3. Add meat, softened chiles, oregano and cumin. Cook, breaking up meat and stirring frequently, until meat is brown.
4. Stir in tomato and onion soups and kidney beans. Bring to a boil and reduce heat. Simmer ½ hour or to desired consistency.

Makes 4 servings.

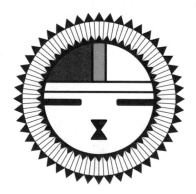

Green Picante Chili

Choose your favorite picante sauce for this easy to prepare dish.

1 tablespoon olive oil
2 pounds lean pork, cut into ½-inch cubes
2 red bell peppers, seeded and chopped
2 white onions, chopped
2 fresh or frozen green chiles, roasted, peeled, seeded, deveined and
    chopped
    OR 1 4-ounce can New Mexico green chiles, drained and chopped
2 jalapeño chiles, seeded and chopped
1 cup water
1 16-ounce jar green picante sauce
3 tablespoons all-purpose flour
½ cup water

1. In a large Dutch oven or heavy pot, heat oil. Add pork cubes a few
    at a time, stirring to brown evenly.
2. Add chopped vegetables. Cover with water and simmer uncovered
    for 1 hour, stirring occasionally.
3. Pour in picante sauce; simmer for 45 minutes to one hour, until
    meat is tender.
4. Blend flour and water together to make a smooth paste. Stir into
    chili mixture and cook for 10 to 15 minutes on low heat.

Makes 6 servings.

Early in September, the Hatch Chile Festival is held in Hatch, New
Mexico. The festival includes a theme parade, sassy food, drinks and
prizes for the best chile.

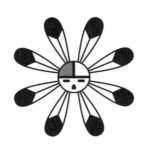

Jalapeño Chili

America's favorite chile pepper adds real heat to this treat. Not for faint of heart.

2 tablespoons vegetable oil
3 pounds lean stew beef, cut into ½-inch cubes
1 pound pork loin, cut into ½-inch cubes
3 large onions, finely chopped
1 tablespoon ground cumin
7 garlic cloves
1 tablespoon ground New Mexico red chile
1 teaspoon Tabasco sauce
2 teaspoons salt
10 jalapeño peppers, seeded and deveined
1 pound fresh or canned tomatoes
sugar to taste
1 12-ounce can beer
1 ounce unsweetened chocolate
4 cups water
½ cup masa harina
½ cup cold water

1. In a large Dutch oven or a heavy pot, heat oil over medium heat. Brown meat. Add onions and cook until soft.
2. In a blender or food processor, blend cumin, garlic, ground chiles, Tabasco sauce, salt, jalapeños and tomatoes. Stop before mixture is pureed. Add to meat and onions.
3. Add sugar, beer and chocolate to mixture; simmer uncovered for 2 hours, stirring occasionally. Add water as necessary to keep chili soupy.
4. One half hour before serving, mix masa with ½ cup cold water to make a paste then add to chili. Stir briskly to thicken chili.
5. During the last half hour of cooking, stir frequently to avoid sticking.

Add salt to taste.

Makes 12 servings

Never Fail Chili

For a novice this is a great way to start cooking chili. It's easy and foolproof—you can't miss with this one.

2 teaspoons vegetable oil
1½ pounds ground beef
1 28-ounce can stewed tomatoes, cored and chopped (reserve 1 cup liquid)
1 medium yellow onion, chopped
1 23-ounce can ranch-style beans
2 tablespoons red chile powder
1 teaspoon ground cumin
1 teaspoon brown sugar
2 teaspoons salt
½ teaspoon garlic powder
3 cups water

1. In a large 4-quart Dutch oven or heavy pot, heat oil. Add beef and cook until brown, stirring frequently. Drain and discard liquid.
2. Add remaining ingredients plus reserved tomato juice. Mix thoroughly and add enough water to make desired consistency. Place on low heat and simmer uncovered for 1 hour.

Makes 6 servings.

In New Mexico, there is an unwritten law that no cowboy can ride his horse on the windward side of the chuckwagon fire in a cow camp. The rule is observed so that no trash or dirt will be stirred up and blown into the kettles or skillets. The chuckwagon cook (know as a Cosi) will run off any green hand who violates this serious breach of manners.

NuMex Big Jim Chili

The use of chocolate in chili is one of Old Mexico's influence on our cooking. Add beans and you have a chili that is definitely different. Try it—you'll like it.

2 tablespoons vegetable oil
1 medium white onion, finely chopped
2 garlic cloves, minced
1 pound lean beef, coarsely ground
½ cup water
1 16-ounce can kidney beans, drained
1 16-ounce can can tomato puree
1 6-ounce can tomato paste
6 Green NuMex Big Jim chiles, roasted, peeled, seeded, deveined and chopped
　　OR 2 8-ounce cans New Mexico green chiles, drained and chopped
1 beef bouillon cube
1 teaspoon ground cumin
2 1-ounce pieces bittersweet chocolate
salt and fresh ground black pepper to taste

1.　In a large Dutch oven or heavy pot, heat oil. Add onion and garlic; cook until onion is soft.
2.　Add meat to the pot. Cook, breaking up with fork and stirring frequently, until meat is brown.
3.　Combine water with kidney beans, tomato puree, tomato paste, green chiles, beef bouillon, cumin and 1 ounce of chocolate. Mix well. Bring to a rolling boil; reduce heat and simmer uncovered for ½ hour. Stir occasionally.
4.　Stir in remaining chocolate and continue cooking until thoroughly blended. Season with salt and pepper to taste.

Makes 2 servings.

Turkey Chili with Anasazi Beans

A new way to use up leftover turkey. It is accompanied by my favorite bean, the Anasazi.

1 pound dry Anasazi beans
6 cups distilled water
3 tablespoons olive oil
1 white onion, minced
3 cloves garlic, minced
2 4-ounce cans New Mexico green chiles, drained and chopped
    OR 3 to 5 fresh or frozen green chiles, roasted, peeled, seeded,
    deveined and chopped
1 tablespoon ground cumin
1 tablespoon dried-leaf oregano
1 teaspoon ground cinnamon
1 pinch cayenne pepper
3 cups chicken broth
4 cups cooked turkey, cut into 1-inch pieces
1½ cup shredded Monterey Jack cheese
salt and fresh ground black pepper to taste
salsa of choice for garnish
sour cream for garnish
minced cilantro for garnish

1. Rinse beans and place in kettle with water. Set aside at least 2 hours and drain before using.
2. In a large Dutch oven or heavy pot, heat oil; add onion and garlic; cook until soft.
3. Add chiles, cumin, oregano, cinnamon and cayenne pepper; cook 3 minutes.
4. Add beans and chicken broth. Bring to boil and reduce heat. Cover and simmer about 2 hours until beans are tender, stirring occasionally.
5. Stir in turkey. Season to taste with salt and pepper. Just before serving, stir in cheese. Heat 1 to 2 minutes until cheese is melted.

Makes 6 servings.

Two-Bean Chili

Not all chili requires long cooking—this one is ready in minutes!

½ pound chorizo sausage
1 medium white onion, chopped
1 14.5-ounce can beef broth
2 15.5-ounce cans red beans, drained and rinsed
1 15.5-ounce can pinto beans, drained and rinsed
2 15.5-ounce cans tomato sauce
2 4-ounce cans New Mexico green chiles, drained and chopped
    OR 6 to 10 fresh or frozen green chiles, roasted, peeled, seeded,
    deveined and chopped
1 tablespoon chili powder
3 teaspoons ground cumin
¼ teaspoon salt
¼ teaspoon fresh ground black pepper
⅛ teaspoon cayenne pepper

1. Remove the casing from chorizo sausage; discard. Crumble sausage.
2. In large Dutch oven or heavy pot, cook sausage and onion until
    onion is soft. Add remaining ingredients; mix well. Cook 10 to 15
    minutes or until thoroughly heated, stirring occasionally.

Makes 6 to 8 servings.

WILD GAME & FRESH FISH

Wild Game

When cooking wild game, it's important to remember that the end results are always determined by the quality of the meat you start with. When you begin with meat of an aged animal, don't expect a tender roast. Hunting for trophies and hunting for food should be considered two different things. When all expenses are considered, the cost per pound of wild game far exceeds the cost of other meats. It only makes sense to be sure that the animal is properly cleaned and cared for before returning home with the meat.

Importance of Preparation

On our homestead we ate a lot of venison. Although New Mexicans generally are referring to deer meat when they use the term venison, venison refers to the meat of deer, antelope, moose or any large antlered animal. Every time I smell venison cooking in the oven, my mind is flooded with memories. Deer meat is much like beef, except the lean part is sweeter and the fat has a much stronger taste. Wild meat is tougher and leaner and needs to be properly aged. Here is an approximate timetable. For best results meat or birds should be kept at 40ºF (5ºC) dry cold if possible. Wild duck and goose should be aged 6 to 8 days; pheasant, 8 to 10 days; rabbit, 2 to 3 days; wild turkey, 6 days; venison, 10 days to 3 weeks. Some meats require further tenderizing, usually accomplished by marinating.

It is sometimes necessary to add fats in the cooking. The recipes I feature here are best when used with meat that has been properly aged. Eating wild game can be an extraordinary experience; it should never be wasted because of poor preparation.

Fresh Fish

Because New Mexico is blessed with abundantly stocked lakes and streams, fishing is very popular in this state. When I go fishing, I always try to keep the fish I catch alive as long as possible. I find that a metal link basket or a live box is much better than a stringer.

The sooner fish are cleaned and cooled, the better they will taste. A quick method is to cut the throat as you would any game animal, remove gills and entrails, wipe the surface, put the fish in a plastic bag and on ice. You can finish the job later. An ice chest with ice is a good way to keep them fresh.

Remember that the digestive juices of fish are strong. If fish are not cleaned promptly they will begin to digest the entrails, causing the flesh on the inside to get soft and off-flavored in the rib area. Bleeding is important, too, because the blood quickly breaks down and seeps into the meat.

Freshly-caught fish should be eaten within a day or two. It can be safely frozen, but the flavor, texture and consistency of fresh fish is far superior. This is why some New Mexico restaurants have their fresh fish flown in daily.

Antelope Barbecue

I know of no better way to prepare the meat of the West's swiftest animal.

3 pounds aged antelope steaks
salt pork or oil
1 cup catsup
1 tablespoon salt (less if you use salt pork)
3 slices fresh lemon
1 white onion, thinly sliced
⅓ cup prepared steak sauce
2 tablespoons tarragon vinegar
1 tablespoon red chili powder

1. Preheat oven to 350°F (175°C).
2. In a large skillet, sear antelope steaks with slices of salt pork or oil, using just enough to keep meat from sticking to pan.
3. In large Dutch oven or heavy pot, place remaining ingredients and bring to a boil, stirring occasionally.
4. Place steaks in a baking pan and cover with sauce. Place pan in oven and bake about 1½ hours, turning occasionally.

Makes 4 servings.

New Mexico's Bureau of Land Management oversees approximately 13 million acres of public lands, which offer a full range of excellent big game hunting. These lands also provide a variety of unusual recreational opportunities, including ski slopes and water activities, such as the Wild Rivers Recreational Area (35 miles north of Taos).

Baked Pheasant & Rice

Pheasant over rice—what a way to enjoy the most beautiful of our game birds!

2 pheasants, cleaned
1 10-ounce can condensed cream of mushroom soup
⅔ cup milk
¾ cup long grain rice, uncooked
½ cup sliced fresh mushrooms
      OR 1 4-ounce can mushrooms, undrained
1 1.5-ounce package dehydrated onion soup
2 tablespoons melted butter
paprika

1.   Cut pheasant into serving pieces
2.   Preheat oven to 325ºF (165ºC)
3.   In a small bowl, blend mushroom soup, milk, rice, mushrooms with juice, and onion soup mix.
4.   Pour mixture into a 13 x 9 x 2-inch baking dish. Arrange pheasant pieces on top. Brush with melted butter and sprinkle with paprika.
5.   Bake uncovered for 1½ hours.

Makes 6 servings.

Braised Rabbit

As a young man, I raised and ate a lot of rabbits. Today we have commercial production of rabbit, and you can find it in the freezer section of your supermarket.

1 young rabbit, cleaned and skinned
1 cup all-purpose flour
2 teaspoons salt, divided
¼ teaspoon ground red New Mexico chile, divided
6 tablespoons shortening
1 cup chicken broth
3 tablespoons lemon juice
6 tablespoons orange juice
1 small white onion, chopped
1 dash ginger
1 cup fresh mushrooms, sliced

1. Cut rabbit into serving pieces. In a bowl combine flour, 1 teaspoon salt and ⅛ teaspoon red chile.
2. Dredge rabbit in flour mixture. Heat shortening in large skillet and sauté rabbit until brown. Reduce heat and drain off excess fat.
3. Add broth, lemon and orange juices, and onion. Season with remaining salt, red chile and ginger. Cover and simmer about 1 hour until tender. Add mushrooms during last 15 minutes of cooking. If desired, thicken juices with seasoned flour.

Makes 4 servings.

Buffalo Tongue

You will be pleasantly surprised with this unusual dish. Leftovers will make delicious sandwiches.

1 buffalo or cow tongue
4 bay leaves
½ teaspoon black peppercorns
1 white onion, chopped
Wild Game Bread Sauce (See p. 179.)

1. In a large saucepan, cover tongue with water. Bring to boil then reduce heat. Add bay leaves, peppercorns and onion. Cover and simmer for 3 to 4 hours until tongue is soft. Add water as necessary. Cool.
2. With a sharp knife, remove and discard skin, fat and bone. Slice meat into thin pieces.
3. Serve warm or cold with Wild Game Bread Sauce.

Serves 6.

American buffalo is now being raised commercially. This elegant animal is really a bison, a shaggy, humped member of the cattle family. The most valued meat from the buffalo is the tongue, which is very tender. It doesn't have a strong gamey flavor; in fact, it tastes a lot like lean beef. Here in New Mexico, media mogul Ted Turner owns the Ladder Ranch and part of the old Armendariz Spanish land grants. He purchased them for raising buffalo and has the largest herd in the state. At last count, there are an estimated 8,000 to 10,000 buffalo in all of New Mexico.

Burgundy Venison Steak Tips

The best of the best. You must try venison in a rich deeply colored sauce.

3 tablespoons oil
2 pounds venison steak, cut into small cubes
2 to 3 tablespoons dry onion soup mix
3 beef bouillon cubes
2 cups water
1 cup Burgundy wine
1 cup fresh mushrooms
    OR 1 4-ounce can mushrooms, drained
3 cups cooked rice

1. In large Dutch oven or heavy pot, heat oil and brown venison.
2. Add remaining ingredients except mushrooms and rice. Cover and simmer for about one hour.
3. Add mushrooms the last 5 minutes.
4. Serve over warm rice.

Makes 6 servings.

Cherokee Venison Meatloaf

Most butchers end up with a lot of ground venison when they cut up your game. I like to use some of it for this meatloaf.

½ cup cornmeal
½ cup water
2 tablespoons oil of choice
1 pound ground venison
1 17-ounce can whole kernel corn, drained
1 small yellow onion, chopped
1 teaspoon salt
2 eggs
Madeira Sauce (See p. 170.)
Wild Rice (See p. 130.)

1. Place cornmeal in a small bowl; add water and blend. Set aside.
2. In skillet heat oil; cook venison until lightly browned. Add corn, onion, salt, eggs and cornmeal-water mixture. Thoroughly combine and cook 3 minutes longer.
3. Preheat oven to 350ºF (175ºC) and grease a loaf pan.
4. Spoon mixture into prepared pan. Bake 35 to 45 minutes. Serve with Madeira Sauce and Wild Rice.

Makes 8 servings.

Venison's natural flavor is sweeter than beef. Tomato sauce, unsweetened berry sauce, vinegar and French dressing complement its rich flavor. Do not overcook—its short fibers toughen quickly if it is overcooked or heated at too high a temperature. Venison is best when it is medium to well done; never serve it rare or overdone.

Duck with Orange

My dad always told me if you shoot it, be prepared to eat it. Duck was a real problem for me until I found this recipe.

2 5-pound ducks, cleaned and plucked, with giblets separated
2 cups water
1 white onion, quartered
¼ teaspoon dried-thyme leaves
½ bay leaf
5 teaspoons salt, divided
½ teaspoon fresh ground black pepper, divided
3 oranges
½ cup white wine
all-purpose flour

1. In a saucepan, cook giblets, necks and wing tips with water, onion, thyme, bay leaf and 1 teaspoon of the salt. Simmer for 45 minutes.
2. Preheat oven to 450°F (230°C).
3. Rub each duck with 1 teaspoon the salt and ¼ teaspoon of the pepper. Cut 1 orange into 8 pieces; place 4 pieces in the cavity of each duck. Place ducks in a baking dish. Prick duck breasts; roast uncovered for 20 minutes.
4. Slice 1 orange very thin and set aside. Shred peel from remaining orange and then juice. Set shredded peel and juice aside.
5. Prick ducks many times again and pour off fat. Cover with orange slices. Reduce oven temperature to 350°F (175°C).
6. In a small bowl, combine wine, orange juice and remaining salt. Pour over ducks and cook for 1 hour. Baste the birds every 10 minutes, turning them to brown evenly. If after an hour they are not brown enough, increase the temperature to 450°F (230°C) and bake 10 minutes longer.
7. Place the ducks on a serving platter and keep warm. Skim fat from the baking dish juices. Add shredded orange peel and 1 cup of strained broth from giblets. Thicken with a flour and water paste. Serve as sauce.

Makes 6 to 8 servings.

Rabbit Stew with Dumplings

Here is how you turn a rabbit into a rich full meal.

1 tablespoon oil
1 large rabbit, cleaned and skinned, cut up
1 large fresh bay leaf
3 sprigs fresh thyme
2 whole cloves
2 onions, chopped
salt to taste
6 peppercorns, crushed
¾ cup water
¾ cup red wine
½ cup diced carrots
12 small boiling onions
12 small mushroom caps
18 small new-red potatoes, peeled
2 tablespoons butter
2 tablespoons all purpose flour
1 tablespoon finely minced cilantro

Dumplings:
1 cup all-purpose flour
2 teaspoons baking powder
salt
1 egg, beaten
½ cup cold milk

1. Heat oil in a large Dutch oven or pot. Lightly brown rabbit. Place bay leaf, thyme and cloves in a cloth spice bag. Add to pot with onions and peppercorns. Salt to taste.
2. Cover with water and red wine; bring to boil. Lower heat, cover and simmer for 2½ hours undisturbed. If sealed well, no additional liquid will need to be added; otherwise, add water as needed.
3. Add diced carrots, boiling onions, mushrooms and potatoes. Cover and cook about 25 minutes until vegetables are tender.
4. While rabbit is cooking, make dumpling mix. In a medium bowl, sift together flour, baking powder and a pinch of salt. Alternately add egg and milk. Mixture makes a stiff batter.
5. Remove spices. In a small bowl combine butter and flour to make a paste. Gradually stir paste into pot, thickening the sauce. Add cilantro and simmer 4 or 5 minutes.

4. Bring to full boil. Drop spoons of dumpling batter into mixture and let them rise. Cover and continue boiling 12 to 15 minutes more, or until dumplings are done.

Makes 4 servings.

Quail in Cabbage Leaves

These little birds dry out so quickly that it is very difficult to cook them and keep their delicate flavor. This old trick works well. Wrapped in the cabbage leaves, they hold their moisture and the spices enhance their wonderful taste.

4 dressed quail
4 cups shredded cabbage
4 slices cooked bacon, crumbled
16 large cabbage leaves
2 tablespoons butter
1 cup chicken stock
4 small apples, cored and sliced
¼ teaspoon dried thyme leaves, crushed
¼ teaspoon dried tarragon leaves, crushed
¼ teaspoon caraway seeds, crushed
1 teaspoon salt
¼ teaspoon fresh ground black pepper

1. Sprinkle each quail with salt and pepper.
2. In a small bowl, combine shredded cabbage and bacon crumbles. Place stuffing in each bird. Wrap each in 4 cabbage leaves; tie with string. Set aside.
3. To make sauce, place remaining ingredients in saucepan; simmer 5 minutes.
4. Place birds in large Dutch oven or heavy pot. Pour sauce over birds. Bring to a boil; reduce heat, cover and simmer 20 to 25 minutes until birds are tender. Remove strings and cabbage leaves, and serve with the sauce.

Makes 4 servings.

Roast Goose

When you are lucky enough to get a goose, you will want to celebrate, and this is a good way to reward yourself. Or you can purchase a frozen goose at the market.

1 4 to 7-pound goose, cleaned and dried
2 teaspoons salt
½ teaspoon fresh ground black pepper

Stuffing:
10 small new red potatoes peeled, quartered
1 tablespoon oil
1 cup onions, chopped
½ cup celery, chopped
¼ teaspoon fresh ground black pepper
1 teaspoon poultry seasoning
4 slices dry bread, crumbed
2 eggs, beaten
1 teaspoon salt

1. Clean and dry goose; rub inside and out with salt and pepper.
2. In a pan place potatoes in water to cover and boil until potatoes are done. Drain potatoes, reserving water for basting. Remove and quarter potatoes.
3. In large skillet, heat oil and sauté onion and celery. Add remaining stuffing ingredients, mix and cool.
4. Stuff goose with mixture and bake 300ºF (155ºC) 3 to 4 hours until goose is done, basting from time to time with reserved potato water.

Makes 4 servings.

Roast Venison

A wine marinade serves a two-fold purpose—it adds a robust flavor and it tenderizes the roast.

2 cups Burgundy wine
1 cup beef bouillon
1 onion, sliced
1 clove garlic, crushed
1 bay leaf
1 6- to 7-pound boneless leg of venison
6 slices salt pork

1. In a large bowl combine wine, beef bouillon, onion, garlic and bay leaf. Place venison in marinade. Cover and refrigerate for 24 hours.
2. Preheat oven to 450ºF (230ºF). Remove meat from marinade, skewer and tie into a roll. Strain marinade and reserve. If meat thermometer is used, insert it in the thickest part of the rolled roast.
3. Place meat on a rack in a shallow roasting pan. Place salt pork slices on top of meat. Roast, uncovered, for 20 minutes. Reduce heat to 325ºF (165ºC) and cook 15 to 18 minutes per pound or to an internal temperature to 140ºF (60ºC) for very rare or 150ºF (65ºC) for medium to well done. Baste occasionally with marinade.
4. Transfer meat to heated serving platter. Remove and discard fat from pan drippings. Strain and serve as sauce.

Makes 8 to 10 servings.

Sandia Rabbit

Curry and wild rice give extra richness to this dish.

1 rabbit, cleaned and skinned
¼ cup olive oil
1 garlic clove
1 cup all-purpose flour
2 teaspoons salt
2 tablespoons dry mustard
1 teaspoon curry powder
1 teaspoon powdered thyme
½ teaspoon fresh ground black pepper
1 cup half and half
2 cups cooked wild rice

1. Cut rabbit into serving pieces. Rub pieces all over with oil, place in bowl, cover and refrigerate overnight. Reserve unused oil.
2. Rub rabbit pieces with cut garlic clove.
3. Combine flour, salt, pepper and spices in a plastic or paper bag. Place rabbit pieces in bag and shake to coat.
4. In large skillet, heat reserved oil; fry rabbit until golden brown and crisp. Reduce heat to simmer; pour in half & half. Cover and simmer 1 hour or until tender. Serve on heated platter over warm wild rice with cream sauce created by added half & half.

Makes 4 servings.

Sweet & Sour Wild Turkey

I don't know any hunter who doesn't remember every detail of his first successful wild-turkey hunt. This noble bird deserves special preparation.

1 6- to 8-pound wild turkey
4 cups water
2 onions, chopped
1 garlic clove, chopped
1 bay leaf
2 whole cloves
½ teaspoon mustard seed
2 teaspoons salt
10 peppercorns
2 tablespoons cornstarch
¼ cup sugar
½ cup vinegar
2 cups cooked wild rice

1. Dress turkey. Cut into serving pieces.
2. Place turkey pieces in a large saucepan or Dutch oven; cover with water. Add onion, garlic, bay leaf, cloves, mustard seed, salt and peppercorns. Bring to boil; reduce heat and cover. Simmer for 2 hours.
3. Remove turkey and strain broth. Return broth to pot. Combine cornstarch, sugar and vinegar and stir into broth. Cook on low, stirring constantly until mixture thickens. Add turkey pieces and simmer for 15 minutes.
4. Serve over warm wild rice.

Makes 4 servings.

For **Baked Turkey**: A wild turkey can be treated the same as a domestic bird. After stuffing the turkey, rub with butter, salt and pepper. Place on a rack in roasting pan. Roast at 325ºF (165ºC). Allow 22 to 25 minutes per pound. Baste the turkey often with equal amounts of butter and white wine.

Venison Au Vin

Hunters are always looking for a way to use stew meat. Pairing with fresh mushrooms and wild rice makes this dish an extra special treat.

¼ pound salt pork
1 pound venison stew meat
½ cup all-purpose flour
1 cup white wine
½ teaspoon salt
½ teaspoon fresh ground black pepper
1 small bay leaf
1 teaspoon parsley flakes
2 white onions, quartered
2 cups potatoes, diced and peeled
3 tomatoes, chopped
2 cups fresh mushrooms
3 cups cooked wild rice

1. In a large skillet, fry salt pork until crisp. Remove meat. Coat venison with flour and brown in hot skillet.
2. Preheat oven to 350ºF (175ºC). In a large Dutch oven or heavy pot, add wine, salt, pepper, bay leaf and parsley. Bring to a simmer; add venison, onions, potatoes, tomatoes and mushrooms.
3. Place in baking pan, cover and bake for about 3 hours. Add wine, if needed to keep moist. Serve over wild rice.

Makes 6 servings.

Venison Jerky

One of the many rewards for a successful hunt is venison jerky. Commercially produced jerky is regaining its popularity as a convenience food for hikers, campers or just an easy, non-messy snack.

4 pounds venison flank steak, partially frozen
6 tablespoon water
6 tablespoons Worcestershire sauce
3 teaspoons salt
6 garlic cloves, minced
¼ teaspoon ground red chile
3 teaspoons ground cumin
4 teaspoons chili powder

1. Trim off all the fat. Slice meat cross grain into long 1/8-inch high and 1-inch wide strips.
2. In a large bowl, whisk together water, Worcestershire, salt, garlic, ground red chile, cumin and chili powder. Add meat strips and coat thoroughly. Tightly cover and marinate 6 hours or overnight.
3. Preheat oven to 200ºF (95ºC). Remove meat and pat with paper towel to remove any excess liquid.
4. Place strips on racks in a foil-lined 9 x 13-inch baking dishes. About 6 racks and dishes will be required. Allow room for air to circulate around dishes. In smaller ovens repeat the process several times until all the strips are dried. Bake about 5 to 6 hours until meat feels dry to touch and is dark brown. Pat with toweling to remove beads of oil. Cool and store in airtight container in refrigerator.
5. If using a dehydrator, place strips in a single layer on a dryer rack. Follow manufacturer's instructions for time and temperature.

Makes 15 to 18 ounces of jerky.

During the settling of the American West, jerky was simply sun-dried lean meat. Today, packaged jerky is not the same as genuine jerky. Most of today's is a pressed by-product made from meat scraps which have been pickled, baked and coated with a smoke flavoring. Homemade jerky made from venison is virtually fat free and greatly superior to commercial beef jerky.

Wild Game Mincemeat

While most mincemeats today do not contain meat, old recipes like this one do. Use mincemeat as filling for pies, tarts, puddings and cookies.

2½ pounds venison stew meat
1 pound beef suet, chopped
½ pound dried currants
2 pounds seedless dark raisins
5 pounds tart apples, coarsely chopped
½ tablespoon cinnamon
½ teaspoon ground allspice
1 teaspoon ground cloves
½ teaspoon freshly ground black pepper
2 teaspoons salt
⅔ cup apple jelly
⅔ cup red currant jelly
2 16-ounce cans tart cherries, undrained and chopped
4 cups apple cider
¾ cup apple cider vinegar

1. In saucepan, cover venison with water and bring to a boil. Reduce heat and simmer until tender. Drain and process in food processor until finely chopped.
2. In a non-reactive saucepan combine remaining ingredients and bring to a boil, stirring frequently. Add venison and boil for 30 minutes, stirring frequently. Cool quickly; pack into freezer containers. This mincemeat can be frozen for up to 4 months.

Makes 8 to 10 cups.

Mincemeat pies: one recipe makes enough for 3 pies. Add 3 tablespoons of brandy to the filling for each pie. Bake double-crusted pies at 425ºF (220ºC) about 40 minutes or until crust is browned and filling is bubbly.

Baked Rainbow Trout

6 rainbow trout
2 teaspoons salt
⅔ cup butter
4 cups soft bread cubes
1 cup fresh mushrooms, sliced
⅔ cup green onions, sliced
¼ cup fresh parsley, chopped
2 tablespoons pimento, chopped
4 tablespoons lemon juice
½ teaspoon dried marjoram leaves

1. Preheat oven to 375ºF (175ºC) and grease a baking dish.
2. Clean, wash and dry trout. Sprinkle 1½ teaspoons salt evenly inside and outside of fish.
3. In a medium skillet, heat ½ cup butter and sauté bread until lightly browned, stirring frequently. Add mushrooms and onions. Cook until tender. Stir in remaining salt, parsley, pimento, lemon juice and marjoram; toss lightly. Cool.
4. Stuff each trout with mixture. Place in a single layer in prepared baking dish. Brush with remaining melted butter.
5. Bake for 15 to 20 minutes or until fish flakes easily.

Makes 6 servings.

Grilled trout: I also like trout rubbed with butter and a little salt, then grilled in aluminum foil.

Crayfish Quiche

If you haven't eaten crayfish (otherwise know as crawdads), you have missed out. Long overlooked, this is a delicate dish you will remember.

48 live crayfish
6 peppercorns
1 bay leaf
4 eggs
1 cup celery, diced
1 cup cheddar cheese, grated
1½ cups mayonnaise
1½ tablespoons Worcestershire sauce
3 tablespoons sherry
1 cup buttered breadcrumbs

1. Preheat oven to 325ºF (165ºC) and butter a baking dish.
2. Rinse crayfish in clean water or soak them for 24 hours in fresh water. Discard any that are dead before cooking.
3. Heat a large pot of water to boiling; add peppercorns and bay leaf. Drop in crayfish and boil 6 to 10 minutes until bright red. Cool and shell. Chop meat.
4. In a bowl, beat eggs until frothy. Add crayfish and remaining ingredients except breadcrumbs.
5. Pour mixture into prepared dish and top with breadcrumbs; bake for one hour. Can be served warm or refrigerated for later use.

Makes 4 servings.

Crawdads, or crayfish, can be found in most shallow unpolluted water. They are caught with traps, a baited line or by hand. They are often used as bait. To transport, place them in a bucket of cool water. A dozen will feed one person.

Fresh Water Bass

Here is a recipe that works for bass, perch, catfish or crappie. All fillet well, and you will find they are delicious. My father used to prepare these this way and every time I fix them it brings back memories of our fishing days. Wonderful memories of great times!

4 freshly caught bass
garlic powder
ground black pepper
salt to taste
1 medium sized white onion, sliced
fresh lemon juice
aluminum foil

1. Preheat oven to 350° to 375°F (175° to 190°C) degrees. Fillet fish using thin knife. Cut down behind gills to backbone, turn knife flat and cut down backbone, stopping just before cutting through skin at tail. Individually place fillets on aluminum foil.
2. Sprinkle with garlic powder, pepper, and salt. Add a few teaspoons of butter around the fish. Place onion rings on top of the fillets. Sprinkle with lemon juice, if you like.
3. Place another piece of foil about the same size as the bottom piece on top of the fillets. Roll the edges to make a large "pocket."
4. Place pockets on cookie sheet in the oven. Bake until done

Serves 4

Any fish that fillets easily can be cooked using this method. It is not recommended for cooking trout because of the bones.

Pecan-Coated Catfish

In New Mexico we have a number of species of catfish and even more ways to catch them. Adults range in size from less than a pound to hundreds of pounds. They can be found in all types of water including ponds, streams, lakes and rivers. Giant catfish put up a very noble fight once hooked. Here is my favorite way to cook these tasty fish.

6 catfish fillets
1 cup pecan halves, toasted and cooled
1 cup buttermilk
2 eggs
1 teaspoon Tabasco sauce or hot sauce of choice
½ cup flour
1 cup yellow cornmeal
1 teaspoon salt
fresh ground black pepper to taste
lemon wedges and parsley sprigs for garnish, optional

1. Place the cooled toasted pecans in a food processor; process until they resemble coarse meal.
2. Rinse the catfish fillets with cold water; pat dry.
3. In a shallow bowl, whisk together the buttermilk, eggs and Tabasco sauce.
4. In a separate shallow bowl or pie plate, stir together the flour, cornmeal, ground pecans, salt and pepper. Dip each fillet into the buttermilk mixture, then into the cornmeal mixture, coating the fillets well. Set aside on waxed paper until ready to cook.
5. Place on a greased pan and bake at 350ºF (175ºC) until browned and fish flakes easily with a fork, about 20 minutes.
6. Serve with lemon wedges and parsley sprigs, if desired.

Makes 6 servings

For **Toasted Pecans**: To toast pecans, spread out evenly in a single layer on a baking sheet. Toast in a 350ºF (175ºC) oven, stirring occasionally, for 10 to 15 minutes. Watch closely, because pecans will burn easily. Be careful not to overcook.

 **SAUCES**

Without sauces many New Mexican dishes would be bland and without soul. Carefully prepared sauces that judiciously use chiles—red or green—are the heart of New Mexico cuisine. Knowledge of chiles and their characteristics determines the quality of the sauces you prepare (See pp. 3–9 for a more complete discussion of chiles). This vegetable has a range of color, heat, and taste that will enhance any dish if properly prepared.

Chile sauces are quite perishable, green more so than red. When I prepare a batch of green chile sauce, I usually fill an ice cube tray and freeze what I don't plan on using, then simply defrost a few cubes the next time I need some. Red sauces can be frozen this way as well.

Red chile sauces are generally made from dried red chile pods or ground red chile. They will keep for a longer period of time than green if refrigerated. Ground chile does not stay at its best for long. After the package is opened, store unused portion in the refrigerator. Whenever possible, use freshly ground chile or chili powder.

I have tried to give you a nice selection of sauces that represent a broad range of tastes. I have also included my favorite wild game sauces. Green sauces have a clearer and sharper taste than red. My selection here includes a basic **Green Chili Sauce** and the somewhat more sophisticated **Tomatillo Green Chile Sauce**, which has a sharper taste. I also offer several red sauces. These are more versatile than green sauces; you can try them all to find the one that you prefer. Some like the hotter **Three Chile Sauce** while others prefer the smoother, richer **Roasted New Mexico Red Chile Cream Sauce**.

Green Chile Sauce

One of the most versatile of New Mexico sauces, this one can be used on a wide variety of dishes. I particularly like this version. You can control the heat by adding or subtracting jalapeño.

2 tablespoons olive oil
¼ cup white onion, finely chopped
1 garlic clove, finely minced
2 tablespoons all purpose flour
½ teaspoon ground cumin
1½ cups chicken broth
1½ cups New Mexico green chiles, roasted, peeled, seeded, deveined and chopped
    OR 2 4-ounce cans of New Mexico green chiles, drained and chopped
¼ teaspoon dried-leaf oregano
1 tablespoon jalapeño chile, seeded and chopped
salt to taste

1. In a 3-quart saucepan, heat oil; stir and sauté onion and garlic. Whisk in flour and cumin. When mixture begins to brown, remove it from heat.
2. Whisking constantly, slowly stir in broth. Add green chiles and oregano. Return to heat.
3. Bring to simmer, stirring frequently. Cover and cook about 10 minutes.
4. Add jalapeño and salt to taste. If a smooth texture is desired, puree in blender or food processor.

Makes 2 cups.

Hot Tomato Sauce

This versatile sauce can be used in a number of dishes. It is especially good for tacos or enchiladas and makes a great dipping sauce. You can easily control the heat by increasing or decreasing the amount of jalapeño peppers you use. I recommend only fresh jalapeños for this recipe. Canned ones just don't seem to taste the same to me.

2 pounds ripe tomatoes
2 tablespoons olive oil
½ cup white onion, chopped
1 garlic clove, minced
1 teaspoon fresh chopped oregano leaves
1 jalapeno chile, seeded and chopped
salt
fresh ground black pepper

1. Rinse tomatoes and core them. Cut in half crosswise; place skin side up on a rack in a roasting pan.
2. Broil 4 to 5 inches from heat until tomatoes are completely blackened. Cool and remove skin, set aside.
3. In a medium skillet, heat oil. Cook onions and garlic until soft. Add tomatoes, oregano and jalapeño pepper.
4. Cook over medium heat for 15 minutes. Cool and place in blender or food processor; puree. Season to taste with salt and pepper.

Makes 3½ cups.

Madeira Sauce

Serve this rich sauce with beef and all red meats. I use Bual or Verdelho, a medium-sweet variety of Madeira. This sauce is often used in expensive restaurant dishes. Try it; you'll like it.

½ cup golden raisins
¼ cup butter
1 tablespoon white onion, minced
3 tablespoons all-purpose flour
2 cups canned condensed consommé, undiluted
⅓ cup Madeira wine
pinch of cayenne pepper

1. Soak raisins 10 minutes in hot water; drain and set aside.
2. In a saucepan, heat butter. Cook onion until golden brown, stirring often.
3. Sprinkle flour over onions and continue to stir about 3 minutes, until blended. Be careful not to scorch the flour.
4. Stir in consommé and continue stirring until mixture thickens.
5. Add raisins, madeira and cayenne. Cook for 1 to 2 minutes. Do not boil. Serve hot.

Makes about 2½ cups.

American-made Madeira is not as distinctive as the Portuguese or Spanish varieties but costs a fraction of the price of the imports.

Mole Sauce

Often called the "National Dish of Mexico," mole (pronounced "mo-lay") has always been popular here in New Mexico. Its taste is a subtle blend of chocolate and chile. The word "mole" comes from the Aztec word *molli*, which means a saucy dish. This dark spicy sauce is used for poultry and includes unsweetened chocolate, which adds a mysterious background.

2 corn tortillas, slightly dried
1 square (1 ounce) unsweetened chocolate
1 garlic clove, chopped
¼ cup blanched almonds
1 small white onion, chopped
2 tablespoons seedless raisins
3 New Mexico green chiles, roasted, seeded, deveined and chopped
    OR 1 4-ounce can green chiles chopped
1 large tomato, quartered
3 tablespoons all-purpose flour
1 teaspoon ground red chile
¼ teaspoon ground cinnamon
¼ teaspoon ground cloves
2½ cups chicken stock

1. Tear tortillas into pieces.
2. In a food processor or blender, add tortilla pieces, chocolate, garlic, almonds, onion, raisins, chiles and tomato; cover and process to a rough puree.
3. Pour into a 3-quart saucepan; stir in flour and spices. Add chicken stock and blend. Bring to a boil; reduce heat. Simmer, uncovered, for 20 minutes, stirring occasionally. The sauce should be the consistency of heavy cream.

Makes 2½ cups.

Chipotle chiles can also be used in mole, but only if you prefer a HOT mole.

Pecos Valley Barbecue Sauce

The moderate temperatures and long pleasant evenings in New Mexico encourage outdoor barbecuing. We also have some of the finest beef available anywhere. This sauce, which comes from the Pecos Valley, is a perfect sauce for beef as well as for basting fish in the oven. I also like this one for chicken.

4 tablespoons butter
1 small white onion, chopped
4 garlic cloves, chopped
2 4-ounce cans New Mexico green chiles, drained and chopped
    OR 8 to 10 fresh or frozen green chiles, roasted, seeded, deveined
    and chopped
1 teaspoon ground paprika
1 teaspoon ground black pepper
¼ cup fresh lemon juice
1 teaspoon dry mustard
½ teaspoon ground red chile
½ teaspoon salt
¼ cup vinegar
1 16-ounce can tomato sauce

1. In medium saucepan, heat butter; add onions and garlic. Cook until onions are soft.
2. Stir in next 7 ingredients; cook over medium heat about 5 minutes. Add vinegar and tomato sauce; bring to boil.
3. Reduce heat and simmer uncovered about 15 minutes until sauce thickens slightly.

Makes 2 to 2½ cups.

Piquant Plum Sauce

Appealingly provocative, this sauce is a good way for you to fully appreciate the term "piquant." An unusual taste treat you must try, it is especially good on all kinds of four-footed or winged wild game.

4 tablespoons sesame oil
3 tablespoons fresh ginger, minced
2 garlic cloves, minced
½ cup wine vinegar
2 pounds ripe purple plums, pitted and halved
4 tablespoons lime juice
½ cup water
2 teaspoons red chile pepper flakes
salt

1. In medium saucepan, heat oil over medium heat; add ginger and garlic. Sauté, stirring constantly, until golden brown, about 1 minute.
2. Add remaining ingredients and simmer 10 to 12 minutes, stirring frequently, until plums are cooked.
3. Cool 10 minutes, then puree in food processor or blender. Use at once or store in refrigerator for up to 3 days. Return to room temperature before serving.

Makes 4 cups.

Red Chile Sauce

If you can't make a good red chile sauce, you can't cook New Mexican style. This is a powerful basic red sauce for those who prefer the richer, fuller taste of the mature red chiles. You can easily adjust the heat by adjusting the amount of ground chile. This can be used in virtually any New Mexico dish. Note that I call for ground chile—NOT chili powder.

2 tablespoons vegetable oil
1 cup white onion, finely chopped
1 garlic clove, minced
½ cup New Mexico ground hot red chile
½ cup New Mexico ground mild red chile
1 can (12 ounces) tomato sauce
6 cups water
salt to taste

1. In a 3-quart saucepan, heat oil; add onions and garlic and sauté until onions are soft. Do not brown.
2. Stir in ground chile, tomato sauce and water. Simmer uncovered until sauce desired consistency. Season lightly with salt.
3. Sauce may be used as is or pureed. Refrigerate in a tightly-covered container or freeze in an ice cube tray.

Makes about 5 cups.

Roasted New Mexico Red Chile Cream Sauce

Another example of why our New Mexican cuisine is gaining in popularity. Hot and rich, this sauce uses fresh chiles and provides a fuller, hotter flavor for those who like to dip appetizers or perk up their enchiladas, burritos or chimichangas. Heat can be adjusted by quantity of chiles used, but I don't recommend the use of canned chiles here.

3 New Mexico red chiles, roasted, peeled, seeded, deveined and chopped
3 serrano chiles, seeded and chopped
4 shallots, minced
3 garlic cloves, minced
2 cups chicken stock
2 cups heavy whipping cream
¾ cup fresh cilantro, chopped
4 medium sorrel leaves, chopped
lemon juice and salt

1. In a saucepan combine the chiles, shallots, garlic, serrano chiles, stock and whipping cream.
2. Bring to a boil; lower heat and simmer until liquid is reduced by half.
3. Pour into food processor or blender. Add cilantro and sorrel leaves and process until smooth. Strain through a fine sieve. Season to taste with lemon juice and salt.

Makes 2½ cups.

Salsa de Chile Rojo

Here's a very Mexican red sauce. The Mexican-style recipes jazz up the spices; this one is typical. Here in New Mexico we tend to use a softer approach, and it's easy to adjust down the amount of oregano and cumin depending on personal preferences. Use this fresh or defrosted, but don't dilute it. The heat element is dependent on the type of chiles used.

6 ounces (about 10 or 12) whole dried red chiles
3½ cups hot water
¼ cup vegetable oil
1 medium onion, chopped (about ½ cup)
2 cloves garlic chopped
1 8-ounce can tomato sauce
1 tablespoon dried oregano leaves
1 tablespoon cumin seed
1 teaspoon salt

1. Cover chiles with warm water. Let stand until softened, about 30 minutes; drain.
2. Strain liquid and reserve
3. Remove stems, seeds and membranes from chiles.
4. In 2-quart saucepan, heat oil. Cook and stir onion and garlic until onion is tender.
5. Stir in chiles, 2 cups of reserved liquid and the remaining ingredients.
6. Heat to boiling; reduce heat and simmer uncovered for 20 minutes and cool.
7. Pour into food processor or blender; cover and process until smooth.

Makes 2½ cups.

Note: This will keep in refrigerator for up to 10 days. It also freezes well. You can use an ice cube tray, then thaw cubes as needed.

San Juan Barbecue Sauce

Barbecue aficionados will appreciate this sauce. Molasses and Liquid Smoke are the keys to its great taste. Use it generously on beef, chicken or pork.

1 tablespoon oil
½ cup yellow onion, finely chopped
1 garlic clove, minced
1 14-ounce bottle ketchup
1 teaspoon Liquid Smoke
6 tablespoons Worcestershire sauce
¼ cup red wine vinegar
2 tablespoons molasses
1 teaspoon dry mustard
⅛ cup ground red chile
¾ teaspoon cumin

1. In a 3-quart saucepan, heat oil; cook and stir onions and garlic until soft.
2. Add remaining ingredients. Simmer uncovered for 15 minutes, stirring occasionally.

Makes 3 cups.

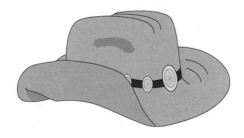

Three Chile Sauce

Fiery is the only way to describe this sauce. Not for amateurs or the faint of heart! If you are looking for a sauce with heat, here's the one to use whenever you want it HOT! See pages 6–8 for further descriptions of these chiles.

4 dried ancho chiles (dried poblanos)
1 chipotle chile (smoked jalapeño)
4 dried cascabel chiles
    OR 1 tablespoon of dried cayenne chile.
3 cups boiling water
¼ cup oil
3 garlic cloves, chopped
1 small white onion, diced
1 tablespoon cumin seeds
1 tablespoon dried-leaf oregano
salt to taste

1. In a bowl, cover the chiles with boiling water. Let stand for 30 minutes or until softened.
2. Strain chiles and reserve liquid. Remove stems and devein.
3. Heat oil in a 2-quart saucepan. Add garlic and onion; stir until onion is tender. Stir in chiles, reserved liquid and remaining ingredients.
4. Heat to boiling; reduce heat. Simmer uncovered 20 minutes; cool.
5. Pour into a food processor or blender; cover and puree. Rub puree through a fine strainer and discard residue. Use immediately or cover and refrigerate for up to 10 days.

Makes 2 cups.

Wild Game Bread Sauce

The cream of the crop in my collection of sauces. Versatile and hearty, it adds that special touch to your wild game.

Basic Brown Sauce:
2 tablespoons butter
1 tablespoon onion, finely chopped
1 teaspoon parsley, minced
2 tablespoons all-purpose flour
1½ cups beef stock
2 tablespoons red wine
salt and fresh ground pepper, to taste

Bread Sauce:
2 teaspoons butter
3 cups dry breadcrumbs
3 cups beef stock
1½ cups minced uncooked ham
1 teaspoon minced shallots
1½ cups basic Brown Sauce
1 tablespoon lemon juice or brandy

Basic Brown Sauce:
1. In a heavy saucepan heat butter. Add onion and parsley and sauté until the onion is soft. Do not brown.
2. Stir in the flour. Cook over medium heat for 1 to 2 minutes, stirring constantly.
3. Heat beef stock and add it to the saucepan, whisking until the mixture is smooth and thickened. Add wine and salt and pepper to taste. Cook for 5 minutes or until slightly thickened.

Bread Sauce:
1. In a saucepan, heat butter. Fry bread crumbs until crisp. Remove crumbs and spread on a paper towel.
2. Add the beef stock, ham and shallots to the butter remaining in the saucepan; simmer for 10 minutes. Stir in Basic Brown Sauce and lemon juice or brandy; simmer 3 to 5 minutes.
3. Just before serving, add the breadcrumbs to the sauce and stir. Spoon over the game when serving.

Makes 8 servings.

SALSA

Salsa was one of the food sensations of the 1990s, and its popularity has continued to climb. Elusively simple in appearance yet complex in composition, salsa is now outselling ketchup, proof that it is becoming America's favorite condiment. The fusion of spices, textures and flavors has brought this New Mexican original to the forefront. Usable as an appetizer, side dish or dessert, its endless variety is making it a part of every cook's presentations.

Sassy or sweet, this taste sensation is only as good as the ingredients you use. Take advantage of the seasons and utilize fresh fruits and vegetables at their peak. Salsa provides you with the chance to experiment and be creative, but be careful—sometimes it is easier to make hot salsa than it is to eat it. If your salsa is too hot, simply add a few drops of vanilla extract. The vanilla will mellow out the salsa and lower the heat sensation.

This group of salsas represents a wide variety of flavors and textures. Use these as a base, and adjust the ingredients to suit your taste. A blender or food processor is essential in the successful preparation of a good salsa. Remember that a great salsa must include an element from at least three of the following categories: spicy/hot, sour/tart, savory, herbal, sweet or aromatic. This will give you the excitement and taste titillation that is making salsa number one.

Apricot Jicama Salsa

I like to use the jicama in salsa because of its slightly sweet flavor and crisp texture. It is a great offset for soft fruit and holds its own with all kinds of fruits and vegetables.

1 medium jicama
4 apricots, pitted and cut into ½-inch strips
2 tablespoons fresh cilantro, minced
½ small red onion, halved and thinly sliced
½ small red bell pepper, seeded, thinly sliced
1 tablespoon dried chipotle chiles, minced
2 tablespoons fresh lime juice
1 tablespoon olive oil
salt and fresh ground black pepper, to taste

1. Using a sharp knife, remove thick outer peel of the jicama.
2. Rinse in cold water and cut into matchstick pieces.
3. In a large plastic or glass bowl, place all ingredients and toss lightly. Refrigerate until ready to serve.

Makes 4 cups.

Blackened Tomato-Mint Salsa

I use a dry skillet to scorch the tomato skins. This creates a smoky undertone without the use of oil. Fresh mint adds a nice touch. Mint is an easy herb to grow in pots or in the open ground.

4 medium ripe tomatoes
1 garlic clove
2 tablespoons fresh lime juice
2 tablespoons vegetable oil
½ teaspoon chili powder
2 New Mexico red chiles, roasted, peeled, seeded, deveined and finely
    chopped
4 tablespoon fresh spearmint leaves, chopped

1. In a large non-stick skillet over high heat, blacken tomatoes by turning them frequently until the skins are scorched.
2. Remove skins and cut tomatoes in half; remove seeds and roughly chop.
3. In a food processor or blender, place tomatoes, garlic, lime juice, oil and chili powder; puree until smooth.
4. In a glass or plastic bowl, combine puree and remaining ingredients. Mix well and refrigerate until ready to serve.

Makes 2 cups.

Fiesta Corn Salsa

New Mexicans make salsa that sets the standard for all to meet. This one is especially good.

1 cup water
½ cup fresh sweet corn kernels
1 red bell pepper, seeded and chopped
½ cup white onion, chopped
2 yellow-wax chile peppers, peeled, seeded and deveined
1 clove garlic, chopped
½ cup chopped fresh cilantro
½ tablespoon tomato paste
½ cup water
⅛ teaspoon cumin
⅛ teaspoon salt

1. In saucepan, bring water to boil. Add corn and blanch 6 to 8 seconds; drain and set aside.
2. Place bell pepper, onion, chile peppers, garlic and cilantro in a food processor. Pulse to chop. Do not puree, salsa should have texture.
3. In a glass or plastic bowl, combine all ingredients. Cover and refrigerate until chilled. Salsa may be stored, covered, 3 days in refrigerator.

Makes 4 servings.

Fresh Basil Salsa

I would not know how to cook if you took away my basil. In the summer I grow it outside and in the winter in a pot in the window. Here is basil at its best.

2 large ripe tomatoes, seeded and cut into ¼ cubes
½ yellow onion, finely chopped
¼ cup fresh basil leaves, chopped
1 serrano chile, seeded and minced
1 teaspoon olive oil
1 teaspoon white-wine vinegar
½ teaspoon fresh lemon juice
¼ teaspoon dry mustard
¼ teaspoon garlic salt
¼ teaspoon lemon pepper

1.   In a bowl, combine tomatoes, onion, basil and chile.
2.   In another small bowl, whisk together oil, vinegar, lemon juice and spices. Pour over vegetables and toss thoroughly. Refrigerate until served.

Makes 2 cups.

Habanero Salsa

Habanero is the hottest chile in the world. Be very careful in handling this pepper. Always wear rubber gloves and keep any of the pepper away from your eyes. This is hot stuff!!

4 cups tomato juice
2 carrots, peeled, blanched and chopped
½ habanero chile, seeded and chopped
1 tablespoon fresh cilantro, chopped
2 garlic cloves, minced
½ teaspoon salt
2 teaspoons honey

1. Place all ingredients in blender and process at high speed until smooth.
2. Taste. If salsa is too hot, add tomato juice as needed. Remember this one is for those who like it HOT.

Serves 6.

Pico de Gallo

If you have ever eaten in a New Mexico restaurant, you have probably been served a version of this treat. The name, which literally means "Rooster's Bill," refers to the old way of eating salad by picking up chunks with your fingers, like a rooster pecks at corn. This is traditionally served with **Fajitas** (See p. 86).

1 cup jicama, peeled and diced
2 ripe tomatoes, seeded and chopped
1 small white onion, finely chopped
6 red radishes, chopped
2 serrano chiles, seeded and finely chopped
2 jalapeño chiles, seeded and finely chopped
½ cucumber, peeled, seeded and chopped
½ cup fresh cilantro, chopped
1 tablespoon fresh lime juice
1 tablespoon fresh lemon juice
1 teaspoon red-wine vinegar
1 garlic clove, minced
½ teaspoon lemon pepper

1. In a glass or plastic bowl, combine jicama, tomatoes, onions, radishes, serrano and jalapeno chiles, cucumber and cilantro.
2. In a small bowl, combine the remaining ingredients. Mix well.
3. Pour contents of small bowl over vegetable and toss. Serve immediately or cover and refrigerate. Best served fresh, with tortilla chips.

Makes 2½ cups.

Pico De Gallo (simplified version)

Simple, colorful, crunchy and delicious, this is a simplified version of the traditional recipe. It can be used as a side dish, salad dressing or dip. I use a little lime juice to enhance the taste, but this addition is optional.

1 tomato chopped
1 white onion chopped
2 cloves garlic
2 jalapenos, seeded and minced
3 teaspoons chopped cilantro
½ teaspoon salt (or to taste)
juice of ½ fresh lime (optional)

1. Combine all ingredients in a glass or non-reactive bowl and let stand for at least 1 hour.

Makes 2½ cups.

Lime Salsa

Zesty and sassy, this salsa will give you a real lift.

8 medium fresh tomatillos
    OR 1 10-ounce can tomatillos
1 large tomato, finely chopped
¼ cup red or yellow bell pepper, minced and seeded
2 tablespoons red onion, minced
1 teaspoon grated lime peel
1 tablespoon lime juice

1. Color of tomatillos should be bright green, not yellow, when skinned. Remove husks and finely chop. If using canned tomatillos, drain and chop in a food processor.
2. Combine tomatillos with all remaining ingredients in a glass or plastic bowl. Cover and refrigerate until chilled. Salsa may be stored 3 days in refrigerator.

Makes 4 servings.

Pineapple Salsa

Light and refreshing fruit salsa is a nice way to start a meal. Try your own blends of fruit and peppers. I like this combination.

2 cups fresh pineapple, chopped
½ cup red bell pepper, seeded and chopped
2 tablespoons New Mexico green chiles, roasted, peeled, seeded, deveined and chopped (if fresh chiles are not available use canned)
2 tablespoons green onions, chopped
1 tablespoon fresh cilantro, chopped
2 teaspoons grated fresh ginger
1 teaspoon lemon peel, grated
½ teaspoon ground cumin
¼ teaspoon salt

1. In a glass or plastic bowl, combine all ingredients.
2. Serve at once or cover and refrigerate until chilled. Salsa may be stored, covered in refrigerator for up to 24 hours.

Makes 2½ cups salsa.

Pumpkin Seed & Avocado Salsa

An unusual combination of texture and tastes, this is one of the best uses for pumpkin seeds I have found.

3 tablespoons shelled pumpkin seeds, roasted
2 ripe avocados
1 serrano chile, seeded
1 tablespoon fresh cilantro, chopped
1 cup fresh parsley leaves
1 tablespoon fresh lemon juice
¼ teaspoon salt

1. In a large skillet, heat pumpkin seeds over medium heat. Stir constantly until toasted, about 5 minutes. Set aside to cool.
2. Cut avocados in half; remove the pits. Peel the halves and chop pulp into small chunks. Place in glass or plastic bowl.

3. In a food processor, coarsely chop pumpkin seeds, chile, cilantro and parsley. Add to avocado with lemon juice and salt. Gently mix with a fork.

Serve immediately.

Makes 2 cups.

Red Bean & Corn Salsa

A few years ago no one would have thought you could use beans in a salsa, but today no one thinks anything about it.

1½ cups frozen corn nibblets. thawed
1 15-ounce can red beans, drained and rinsed
1 green bell pepper, seeded and diced
1 yellow or red bell pepper, seeded and diced
2 medium tomatoes, diced
½ cup white onion, diced
3 jalapeños, seeded and diced
⅓ cup fresh lime juice
⅓ cup vegetable oil
⅓ cup cilantro, chopped
1 teaspoon salt
½ teaspoon ground cumin
½ teaspoon ground red New Mexico chile

1. In a glass or plastic bowl, combine all the ingredients and refrigerate for at least 3 hours. Serve with tortilla chips.

Makes 3 to 4 cups.

I use red beans in this one. If you prefer, use black beans. I also use olive oil instead of vegetable for a little change of pace.

Red Grapefruit Salsa

Tangy colorful red grapefruit combined with a few ingredients result in an outstanding salsa.

2 ruby red grapefruits
½ cup white onion, diced
1½ tablespoons New Mexico green chiles, roasted, seeded, deveined and
    chopped
2 tablespoons fresh cilantro, chopped
¼ teaspoon cumin

1. Peel grapefruit and cut into segments, removing all white pith.
    Chop segments.
2. In a glass or plastic bowl, combine all ingredients. Serve at room
    temperature, or cover and refrigerate. Use within 24 hours.

Makes 2 cups.

Simple Salsa

Here is a quick easy salsa recipe.

4 tomatoes, peeled and chopped
½ cup white onion, minced
½ cup celery, minced
¼ cup green or red bell pepper, seeded and minced
¼ cup virgin olive oil
1 4-ounce can New Mexico green chiles, drained and chopped
    OR 3 to 5 fresh or frozen green chiles, roasted, peeled, seeded,
    deveined and chopped
2 tablespoons red wine vinegar
1 teaspoon mustard seed
1 teaspoon ground coriander
1 teaspoon salt
dash of fresh ground black pepper

1. In a glass or plastic bowl, combine all ingredients. Cover and refrigerate for at least 3 hours.
2. Serve with tortilla chips or use as mild sauce for other dishes.

Makes 2 cups.

Sweet Melon-Jicama Salsa

Crunchy jicama is blended with melons to create a sweet taste that contrasts with the heat of the jalapeño pepper.

1 cup honeydew melon, peeled, seeded and chopped
1 cup cantaloupe melon, peeled, seeded and chopped
1 jalapeño chile, seeded and chopped fine
½ cup jicama, peeled and chopped
1 tablespoon fresh ginger, chopped fine
2 tablespoons fresh cilantro, chopped fine
2 tablespoons lime juice

1. In a glass or plastic bowl combine all ingredients.
2. Serve at once or cover and refrigerate until chilled. Salsa may be stored, covered in refrigerator for 2 hours.

Makes 2½ cups.

Tomatillo Green Chile Sauce (*salsa verde*)

The development of sauces like this one will keep our style of cooking in the forefront of American cuisine for years to come. Here's a citric sauce that you can use as a dip for chips; use whenever you want a tart green sauce.

½ pound fresh tomatillos
    OR 2 13-ounce cans, drained
2 canned serrano chiles, rinsed and seeded
    OR 1 fresh serrano chile, seeded.
2 tablespoons fresh cilantro, chopped
½ small white onion, chopped
1 garlic clove, chopped
1½ teaspoons oil
½ cup chicken stock
Salt to taste

1. Remove husks from tomatillos and chop. Color should be bright green, not yellow.
2. In small saucepan, place tomatillos and chiles; add water to cover. Bring to boil; reduce heat and simmer about 10 minutes until tender.
3. Remove tomatillos and chiles with slotted spoon and cool.
4. In a food processor or blender, place all ingredients except oil and chicken stock. Pulse to a coarse puree.
5. Heat oil in medium skillet. Add puree and cook, stirring constantly, about 5 minutes or until mixture darkens and thickens.
6. Add chicken broth; bring to boil. Reduce heat and simmer until the mixture thickens slightly. Season with salt to taste.

Serve warm.

Makes 4 servings.

Tomatillos are little green, tomato-like vegetables with parchment skin. Their pulp is very dense, and they have tiny seeds. Select brilliant green ones for the best tartness.

Tomatillo Salsa

Use brilliant green tomatillos for best flavor and tartness.

8 fresh tomatillos, husks removed, rinsed and diced
2 medium-sized tomatoes, peeled, seeded and diced
1 medium-sized cucumber, peeled, seeded and diced
1 small white onion, diced
1 serrano chile, seeded and chopped
2 tablespoons of white wine vinegar
6 tablespoons of olive oil
1 teaspoon of sugar
1 teaspoon dry mustard
½ teaspoon dry basil
¼ teaspoon of salt
⅛ teaspoon fresh ground black pepper

1. In a glass or plastic bowl, combine tomatillos, tomatoes, cucumber and chile.
2. In another small bowl, whisk together the remaining ingredients. Pour over the vegetables and toss thoroughly. Refrigerate until served.

Serves 4.

Tomato Salsa

Also known as *salsa cruda*, this is one of my favorites. If you raise your own tomatoes, as I do, use them to make this especially great.

6 ripe tomatoes, chopped
½ cup white onion, chopped
½ cup green onions, chopped
2 garlic cloves, minced
1 jalapeño chile, seeded and chopped fine
1 tablespoon olive oil
1 tablespoon wine vinegar
½ cup fresh cilantro, chopped
1 teaspoon dried-leaf oregano
1 teaspoon salt
½ teaspoon fresh ground black pepper

1. In glass or plastic bowl, combine all ingredients.
2. Cover and refrigerate for at least 4 hours before serving.

Makes 3 to 4 cups.

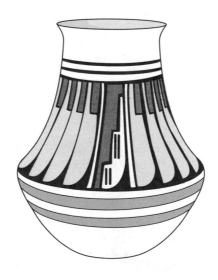

DESSERTS

For those who would like to try a real fiery dessert, **Hot Chocolate Cake** combines the habanero chile and chocolate. Because it's not for the novice—watch out. For something more traditional, treat yourself to the **Sopa Indian Bread Pudding**. If you like pumpkin pie that's a little different, **Pecos Valley Pumpkin Pie** with a butterscotch-cream sauce is one you should try. Serve it for your next party and expect compliments. An unexpected use of tortillas results in the delicious **Banana and Pineapple Tortilla Dessert**. **Rum Apple Crisp** will be appreciated by both family and guests. Eve Ware is one of the most extraordinary cooks I know. She gave me her recipe for **Eve's Pear Tart**. Please prepare this delicacy; it's as special as the lady who shares it with us.

High altitude baking: Altitude can have an effect on cooking, particularly baking. For a discussion of baking at high altitudes, see "Altitude Adjustments" on pages 241–43 in the Appendix.

Eve's Pear Tart

You have never tasted pears like these. From Eve Ware, a great cook.

Crust:
1¾ cups all-purpose flour
¾ cup cold butter, cut into ½-inch pieces
¼ cup sugar
2 egg yolks
1 teaspoon water
1 teaspoon vanilla extract

Filling:
1 cup plus 3 tablespoons sugar
6 tablespoons all-purpose flour
3 eggs
¾ cup (1½ sticks) butter
2 Bartlett pears, peeled, cored and quartered lengthwise
powdered sugar for garnish

Crust:
1. In a food processor, combine flour, butter and sugar. Pulse about 45 seconds, until mixture resembles coarse meal. Add yolks, water and vanilla; process until crumbly.
2. Turn dough out and shape into a ball. Flatten slightly, wrap in plastic and freeze 20 minutes or refrigerate overnight.
3. Knead dough slightly; do not overwork. On a lightly-floured surface, roll dough into a 13-inch circle.
4. Press dough into an 11-inch tart pan or glass pie plate; trim excess dough. Crimp edges. Refrigerate 15 minutes.

Filling:
1. In a bowl combine sugar, flour and eggs until smooth.
2. In a sauce pan, melt butter until foamy. Slowly whisk melted butter into sugar mixture. Set aside.

To Assemble:
1. Preheat oven to 375ºF (190ºC).
2. Cut pears lengthwise into ⅛-inch thick slices. Gently open slices into a fan shape. Arrange pears in crust in flower pattern. Pour filling over pears. Bake about 1 hour until brown. Sprinkle with powdered sugar.

Makes 6 generous servings.

Chocolate Tortilla Dessert

Have you tried using tortillas in a dessert? This presentation gives you the opportunity to use them in an unusual way.

1½ pounds sweet chocolate
¾ cup butter
1½ cups half-and-half cream
½ cup powdered sugar
3 ounces brandy
18 flour tortillas
vegetable oil
¾ cup granulated sugar
¼ cup ground cinnamon

1. Melt chocolate and butter in top of double boiler and stir until smooth. Add half-and-half and powdered sugar. Heat until sugar is dissolved, stirring continuously. Stir; remove from heat and add brandy. Keep warm in fondue pot or chafing dish and set aside.
2. Cut each tortilla into 8 wedges. Heat oil in heavy skillet or deep fryer to 350ºF (175ºC). Fry tortilla chips, being careful not to crowd them. Remove with slotted spoon and drain well.
3. Combine granulated sugar with cinnamon. Put in shaker. Sprinkle chips with cinnamon sugar and powdered sugar if desired.
4. Place in basket and serve with chocolate sauce for dipping.

Makes 12 servings.

Hondo Raisin Cream Pie

Hidden under the meringue is a creamy-rich filling.

Crust:
1 cup all-purpose flour
½ teaspoon salt
⅓ cup shortening
3 to 4 tablespoons cold water

Cream filling:
3 egg yolks, slightly beaten
1½ cups sour dairy cream
¾ cup sugar
¼ cup all-purpose flour
1 teaspoon ground cinnamon
¼ teaspoon ground cloves
1 cup raisins
½ cup pecans, chopped

Meringue:
3 egg whites
¼ teaspoon salt
¼ teaspoon cream of tartar
6 tablespoons sugar

Crust:
1. Preheat oven to 450ºF (230ºC).
2. In large bowl, mix together flour and salt. Using a pastry blender or 2 knives, cut in shortening until the size of small peas. Sprinkle cold water over mixture, stirring lightly until dough holds together.
3. Shape into a ball, flatten to ½-inch thickness. On a lightly floured surface, roll dough into a 9½-inch circle. Press into an 8-inch pie pan. Fold edges and crimp. Prick generously with fork.
4. Bake 10 to 12 minutes. Cool.

Filling:
1. In top of double boiler, blend egg yolks and sour cream; stir in sugar, flour, cinnamon and cloves.
2. Cook over hot water until mixture thickens, stirring occasionally. Stir in raisins and pecans. Cover and cool.

Final assembly:
1. Preheat oven to 350ºF (175ºC).
2. Make meringue: In a bowl, beat egg whites, salt and cream of tartar until slightly mounding. Gradually beat in sugar. Beat until meringue is stiff and glossy.
1. Turn filling into baked pie shell. Top with meringue, sealing at edge of crust.
2. Bake for 10 to 15 minutes. Cool before serving.

Makes one 8-inch pie.

Hot Chocolate Cake

The ultimate hot dessert. Try this before serving to guests; it is strictly for those who like food HOT!!!!

Cake:
4 dried habanero chiles
1 cup boiling water
6 tablespoons unsweetened cocoa powder
1 teaspoon baking powder
½ teaspoon baking soda
1 teaspoon vanilla extract
½ cup shortening
2 cups sugar
3 eggs
2 cups cake flour
½ teaspoon salt
½ cup buttermilk

Frosting:
¼ cup milk
¼ cup butter
1 ounce unsweetened chocolate, melted
2½ cups powdered sugar
½ teaspoon vanilla
¼ cup pecans, finely chopped
ground red chile

1. Preheat oven to 350ºF (175ºC). Grease and flour a 13 x 9-inch pan.
2. Boil chiles in water for 10 minutes. Set aside (this can be done ahead of time). After 30 minutes, strain chiles through fine mesh and remove as much pulp as possible. Pour the chile water in a measuring cup. Add enough hot water to make 1 cup.
3. In a bowl, blend chile water and cocoa powder into a smooth paste. Stir in baking powder, soda and vanilla; set aside.
4. In mixing bowl, beat shortening and sugar. Add eggs, 1 at a time, beating after each addition. Sift flour and salt into a small bowl. Add alternately with buttermilk, using low speed. Add cocoa mixture; beat until smooth.

5. Pour into prepared pan; spread evenly to edges. Bake 35 minutes or until cake springs back when lightly pressed.
6. Cool 10 minutes in pan, then turn out cake onto rack. Cool.

Frosting:
1. In a saucepan heat milk, butter and chocolate until mixture boils. Remove from heat.
2. Beat in powdered sugar and vanilla until smooth and creamy. If too thin, let cool slightly; if too thick, add a few drops of milk. Frost cake while frosting is still warm. Sprinkle with pecans and lightly dust with chile powder.

Makes one 13 x 9-inch cake.

The Yucatan habanero chile is 30 to 50 times hotter than the jalapeño. Be careful handling this chile. In spite of its intense heat, it has a very distinctive, tropical flavor. The ripe fruit is sweeter than the green and has a more mature fruitiness. Closely related to the Scotch bonnet chile, it is becoming very popular in the U.S.

Layered Banana & Pineapple Tortilla Dessert

Another example of how versatile the tortilla can be. Here its wafer-like crispness contrasts with two creamy-fruit fillings.

5 8-inch flour tortillas
4 tablespoons butter

Pineapple filling:
1 20-ounce can crushed pineapple with juice
1 tablespoon rum
2 egg yolks
1 tablespoon cornstarch
2 tablespoons sugar
½ cup roasted almonds, coarsely chopped, blanched

Banana filling:
1½ cups whipping cream
1 tablespoon rum
½ cup sugar
¼ cup flour
2 whole eggs
2 egg yolks
2 sliced bananas
whole strawberries
whole blanched almonds

1. Preheat oven to 325F (165C). Butter both sides of tortillas. Place on cookie sheets; bake about 20 minutes until crisp, turning 2 to 3 times. Cool.

Pineapple filling:
1. In a saucepan, combine all ingredients except almonds. Heat slowly to boiling as mixture thickens; continue slowly boiling for 3 minutes. Remove and chill. Stir in almonds before using.

Banana filling:
1. In a saucepan, bring the cream and rum to a boil; set aside. In double boiler, over hot boiling water, beat sugar, flour, eggs and egg yolks until light. Slowly add cream-rum mixture, beating continually until mixture thickens enough to hold its shape. Remove from heat and cover. Chill; add bananas before using.
4. Place a spoonful of banana filling in center of each serving plate. Form a stack by alternating filling and tortillas, ending with a tortilla on top. Garnish with strawberries and almonds. Cut into 6 individual servings and serve immediately.

Makes 6 servings.

Honey & Spice Cupcakes

Delicious and easy to make, this is a modern version of an old ranch recipe that was a favorite of my uncle Ray.

⅓ cup butter
½ cup packed brown sugar
1 egg
¾ cup applesauce
1½ cups all-purpose flour
1 cup rolled oats
1 teaspoon ground cinnamon
1 teaspoon baking soda
1 teaspoon salt
½ teaspoon ground nutmeg
½ cup milk

Honey Glaze:
2½ cups powdered sugar
2 tablespoons milk
1 teaspoon orange juice
2 tablespoons honey
coconut

1. Preheat oven to 375°F (190°C). Grease 12-cup muffin tin.
2. In bowl, cream together butter and brown sugar. Beat in egg and applesauce.
3. In small bowl, combine flour, oats, cinnamon, soda, salt and nutmeg. Blend into creamed mixture alternately with milk.
4. Pour batter into prepared cups, filling each ¾ full. Bake 20 to 22 minutes. Cool.
5. In small bowl, combine glaze ingredients except coconut and beat until smooth. Spread on cupcakes. Sprinkle with coconut.

Makes 12 muffins.

Rolled oats in my recipe refers to old-fashioned oats, not the quick type. If you only have the quick-cooking type, they can be substituted.

Pecan Peach Cake

A delicious cake! Roast pecans lend a marvelous flavor. I've always been fond of peaches, and this is my all-time favorite peach cake.

2 large peaches, peeled and cut into slices
3 tablespoons packed brown sugar
1 tablespoon lemon juice
3 eggs, separated
⅔ cup sugar
2 cups pecans, roasted and finely ground
⅓ cup all-purpose flour
1 teaspoon orange zest, minced
¼ teaspoon salt
3 egg whites
2 tablespoons unsalted butter, cut into small pieces
whipped cream for garnish

1. Preheat over to 350ºF (175ºC). Generously butter and lightly flour a 9½ x 3 or 10 x 3-inch springform pan.
2. In a bowl, toss the peaches gently with brown sugar and lemon juice.
3. In another small bowl, beat the egg yolks and sugar until pale yellow and fluffy. Separately combine pecans, flour, zest and salt. Stir into egg and sugar mixture.
4. Beat egg whites until stiff but not dry, gently fold into batter. Pour into prepared pan.
5. Drain peaches and place in a circle on top of batter; dot with butter.
6. Bake 35 to 40 minutes, or until a wooden pick comes out clean. Cool on rack. Open pan and serve topped with whipped cream.

Makes 8 servings.

Pecos Valley Pumpkin Pie

A delicious butterscotch sauce makes this a special treat.

⅔ cup sugar
1 cup cooked pumpkin
¼ teaspoon salt
¼ teaspoon ground ginger
¼ teaspoon ground mace
½ teaspoon ground cinnamon
2 large eggs, beaten slightly
1 cup milk
1 tablespoon melted butter
1 unbaked 8-inch pie crust, (For recipe, see page 198, **Hondo Raisin Cream Pie**)

Butterscotch Sauce:
½ cup plus two tablespoons packed brown sugar
⅓ cup dark corn syrup
2 tablespoons butter
6 tablespoons half-and-half
1 cup heavy whipping cream
½ teaspoon vanilla extract
½ teaspoon rum flavoring

1. Preheat oven to 450ºF (230ºC). In large bowl, combine sugar, pumpkin, salt, ginger, mace and cinnamon. Add eggs and mix well. Stir in milk and butter.
2. Pour into unbaked pie crust; bake for 10 to 12 minutes. Reduce heat to 400ºF (205ºC); bake for 5 minutes. As crust browns reduce heat to 300ºF (150ºC). Bake until knife tip inserted in center comes out clean, about 45 to 55 minutes.

Serve with butterscotch sauce.

Butterscotch Sauce:

1. In saucepan, combine brown sugar, syrup and butter. Bring to a boil, stir constantly until mixture reaches 234ºF (112ºC) or until a small amount dropped into cold water forms a soft ball. Remove from heat immediately and pour in half & half. Beat thoroughly, adding vanilla and rum flavoring. Set aside and cool to room temperature.
2. In mixing bowl or copper bowl, whip heavy cream until just stiff. Fold 4 tablespoons of butterscotch sauce into whipped cream; refrigerate until serving.
3. Serve remaining sauce and flavored whip cream as separate items with the pie.

Makes one 8-inch pie.

Ruidoso Downs Pie

This a New Mexico version of the famous **Kentucky Derby Downs Pie**. A sure way to please your guests before heading to the races.

Crust:
1 cup all-purpose flour
¼ teaspoon salt
⅓ cup shortening
2 to 3 tablespoons cold water

Filling:
½ cup butter
1 cup sugar
½ cup all-purpose flour
2 eggs
1 teaspoon vanilla extract
1 cup semi-sweet chocolate chips

whipping cream

1. In mixing bowl, mix flour and salt. Using a pastry blender or 2 knives, cut in shortening until it resembles a coarse meal. Add water; mix together and shape into a ball. Wrap in plastic wrap and refrigerate for at least 20 minutes.
2. Preheat oven to 375ºF (190ºC). On a lightly floured surface, roll dough into a 10-inch circle. Pat and fit into a 9-inch pie plate; fold edges and crimp; set aside.
3. Beat together filling ingredients except for whipping cream. Pour into pie crust; bake 30 to 40 minutes. Do not overcook. Cool and serve topped with whipped cream.

Makes 8 servings.

Rum Apple Crisp

Rum and lemon combined with apple create a new flavor sensation.

Topping:
½ cup pecans, coarsely chopped
⅓ cup packed brown sugar
½ cup all-purpose flour
½ cup butter
½ cup shredded coconut

Filling:
2 pounds cooking apples
¼ cup golden raisins
¼ cup packed brown sugar
¼ cup all-purpose flour
¼ cup rum
3 tablespoons lemon juice
1 teaspoon grated lemon peel

ice cream, whipped cream or sour cream as accompaniment

1. In a food processor or blender, combine nuts and sugar and process well. Add flour and butter; process until well mixed. Stir in coconut and set aside.
2. Preheat oven to 400°F (205°C). Grease 12 x 7 x 2-inch baking dish.
3. Peel, core and thinly slice apples. In a bowl, toss apples with remaining ingredients. Spoon mixture into prepared baking dish. Cover with crisp topping.
3. Bake 35 to 45 minutes until topping is well browned and bubbling. Serve warm with ice cream, whipped cream or sour cream.

Makes 8 servings.

Sopa Indian Bread Pudding

Here is a very good way to use your stale bread. Like all bread puddings, it is very rich and satisfying.

1 loaf white sandwich bread
1 12-ounce package American cheese, sliced
1 cup pecans, chopped
1 15-ounce package seedless raisins
2½ cups water
3 cups packed brown sugar
1 tablespoon ground cinnamon
¼ teaspoon ground nutmeg
1 tablespoon butter
cream

1. Lightly toast bread and tear in pieces. In a 2 quart baking dish, put a layer of pieces. Place sliced cheese in a layer over the bread pieces. Sprinkle pecans and raisins over cheese; fill as full as possible, pressing down if necessary.
2. Preheat oven to 350ºF (175ºC). In a saucepan, heat water, brown sugar, cinnamon, nutmeg and butter. Bring to a boil then reduce heat; simmer for 15 minutes. Pour over mixture until all ingredients are soaked and covered. Cover dish with foil; bake for 1 hour. Serve warm or cold, plain or with cream.

Makes 8 servings.

The Spaniards brought a number of items to Native Americans of New Mexico. These include the wheel, metal tools, a written language and gunpowder. They changed the Indians' diet by introducing fruit trees, wheat, sheep, pigs, horses and many vegetables.

Sopapillas

Often referred to as little pillows of pleasure, sopapillas are a standard item in almost all New Mexican restaurants. They are offered hot with honey as a desert—or stuffed with meat of choice and served with refried beans, guacamole, shredded cheese, Spanish rice and shredded lettuce. Here is the basic recipe for sopapillas served as a dessert. Try these—they are well worth your effort.

1 package dry yeast
¼ cup lukewarm water
¾ cup milk
6 tablespoons sugar
1 teaspoons salt
2 tablespoons butter
1 egg, beaten
3 cups flour
honey
approximately 2 inches cooking oil

1. In a small bowl, soften yeast in lukewarm water. Set aside.
2. In a one-quart saucepan, combine milk, sugar and salt. Bring to a boil. Remove from heat. Stir in butter. Allow to cool until lukewarm.
3. Stir in beaten egg and yeast mixture. Gradually add flour. Work with hands, if mixture becomes too thick to stir.
4. Cover dough with a damp cloth and allow to rise until doubled in size, about 1½ hours.
5. Punch down; turn out onto a lightly floured board and knead briefly until dough is smooth.
6. Cover and let rest for additional 15 minutes. Roll to about ½ inch thick square and cut into triangle or rectangle shapes.
7. Heat oil to 350°F. Cook sopapillas a few at a time, browning on one side and turning only once. They will puff up.
8. Drain on absorbent paper towels and serve. Most New Mexicans bite off a corner and dribble honey inside to eat.

Makes 8 to 10

COOKIES & CANDIES

Once again I take you back to my childhood with recipes handed down through generations of New Mexican cooking. Featured here are the best of dozens of the many variations I have found. You will like my choices.

Pecans and peanuts are the two ingredients found most often in New Mexico homemade cookies. You will be surprised at how well orange and pecan combine for **Mexican Orange Candy**. Especially delightful each fall, when the new Valencia peanut crop becomes available, are **Portales Peanut Patties**. These are quick and easy and are great eating.

Also included is an old ranch recipe for **Carrot Cookies**. One of the easiest to make and best-tasting cookies in my collection, this old family recipe comes straight off the homestead and is as good today as it was 50 years ago when I first tasted one. The only change in this old recipe is the cream cheese frosting I have added.

Each year at Christmas, cookies like **Biscochitos**, **Empanditas** and **Bunuelos** come out of the ovens all over New Mexico. I always look forward to the appearance of these special treats.

Biscochitos

New Mexico was the first state in the nation to have an official cookie. The biscochito was declared our official State Cookie in 1989. These beloved little anise-flavored cookies are very popular here. Treasured Spanish family recipes have been handed down for generations, and biscochitos are made for every special occasion, most importantly Christmas. This recipe was given to me years ago by Nellie Fields, a great cook.

2 cups lard or shortening
1 cup sugar
1 teaspoon anise seed
2 eggs
6 cups sifted flour
3 teaspoons baking powder
1 teaspoon salt
¼ cup water or dry sherry or white wine
½ cup sugar
1 teaspoon cinnamon

1. Preheat oven to 350°F (175°C). In a mixing bowl, cream shortening thoroughly. Add sugar and anise seed. Add eggs to mixture and beat until fluffy.
2. In separate bowl, sift flour and add baking powder and salt.
3. Add dry mixture to first bowl. Add water and knead until well mixed.
4. On a lightly floured board, roll to ¼-inch thick. Cut into fun shapes or put through cookie press. Mix the cinnamon and sugar and sprinkle tops of cookies. Bake until light brown.

Yields 4 to 6 dozen cookies

Bunuelos

These are nicknamed mini sopapillas or New Mexican doughnuts. Make a large batch—they seem to disappear.

Topping:
1 cup sugar
2 teaspoon cinnamon

Bunuelos:
1½ cups all-purpose flour
1 tablespoon sugar
1 teaspoon baking powder
½ teaspoon salt
1 egg, lightly beaten
¼ cup water
1 tablespoon melted butter
vegetable oil for frying, at least 1½ inches deep

1. In a small dish, combine 1 cup sugar and cinnamon; set aside for topping.
2. In mixing bowl, combine flour, sugar, baking powder and salt. Add egg and water and mix until smooth.
3. On a floured surface, knead dough gently until soft. Brush with melted butter. Place dough in bowl, cover and let rise until doubled.
4. Turn dough out, punch down and divide into 6 pieces. Roll out each piece on a lightly floured surface until very thin. Slice each piece into 4 long rectangles; let stand 5 minutes.
5. In large skillet or deep fryer, heat oil. Fry until golden brown, turning once. They will puff up like little sopapillas. Remove with tongs and drain on paper towels. While still warm, coat with reserved sugar and cinnamon.

Makes about 24 bunuelos.

Carrot Cookies

This old recipe is a hand-me-down from my great aunt. If you like carrot cake, you will love these cookies.

2 cups all-purpose flour
1 tablespoon baking soda
½ teaspoon salt
1 teaspoon allspice
1 teaspoon ground cinnamon
½ teaspoon nutmeg
½ cup shortening
¼ cup sugar
¾ cup honey or maple syrup
2 eggs
1 cup carrots, peeled and grated
2 cups rolled oats
1 cup raisins
1 cup pecans, chopped
3 teaspoons vinegar

Frosting:
1 3-ounce package cream cheese, softened
¼ cup butter, room temperature
½ teaspoon vanilla extract
2 cups powdered sugar

1. Preheat oven to 375ºF (190ºC). Grease cookie sheet.
2. In a bowl sift together flour, soda, salt and spices.
3. In another bowl, cream shortening and sugar; add honey or syrup and eggs. Beat well. Add carrots, oats, raisins, nuts, dry ingredients and vinegar. Stir to blend.
4. Drop by teaspoons onto prepared cookie sheets. Bake 20 minutes.

Frosting:
1. In a mixing bowl, blend cream cheese, butter and vanilla until well blended. Add sugar; beat until smooth. Frost top of each cookie.

Makes 36 to 40 cookies.

Empanadas or Empanaditas

Like their cousins the turnovers, empanadas (or their smaller versions—empanaditas) can be filled with an endless variety of fruits and meats. These tasty treats can be served hot or cold.

Filling:
2 cups apples, peeled and diced
¾ cup sugar
½ teaspoon ground cinnamon
⅛ teaspoon nutmeg
1 teaspoon cornstarch
½ tablespoon fresh lemon juice
1½ tablespoons butter
oil for frying

Pastry:
2 cups all-purpose flour
½ teaspoon salt
½ teaspoon baking powder
¼ teaspoon ground cloves
¼ teaspoon ground cinnamon
2 tablespoons butter
6 tablespoons cold water
powdered sugar

1. In 2-quart saucepan, combine all ingredients and cook until apples are tender and mixture is thick (about 1 hour). Set aside.
2. Place all pastry ingredients except water in bowl of food processor and blend 6 seconds or until a coarse meal is obtained. Stop, sprinkle water over mixture and process a few more seconds to incorporate, but stop before it forms a ball.
3. Place dough in bowl and gently knead and form into a ball. Place the ball of dough in a plastic bag and chill for 20 minutes.

4. Roll out dough on a lightly floured surface to a thickness of ⅛-inch. Cut into 3-inch rounds for small empanaditas or 4½-inch rounds for larger ones (empanadas). Place a spoonful of filling in the center of each; moisten edges with water. Fold over into half-moon; press edges together, crimp with fork tines. Turn over and crimp other side. Set aside.
5. In a deep skillet or deep fryer heat oil to 375ºF (190ºC). Drop in empanadas or empanaditas and fry 2 to 4 minutes until brown on both sides. Drain on paper toweling, cool briefly and sprinkle with powdered sugar.

Makes 6 empanadas or 9 empanaditas.

In 1990, after a long battle, 7,100 acres northwest of Albuquerque, New Mexico, were finally designated as Petroglyph National Monument. The new park includes 5 extinct volcanoes, thousands of petroglyphs and numerous Native American shrines. Prehistoric people created the snakes, birds, lightning patterns, masked figures and animals that still decorate the ancient black lava rock.

New Mexico Wedding Cookies

One of the reasons so many children look forward to weddings are these little cookies. They are traditional at weddings in New Mexico.

1½ cups butter
¾ pound powdered sugar
1 egg yolk
1 teaspoon vanilla extract
½ cup almonds finely chopped
3¼ cups all-purpose flour

1. Preheat oven to 275°F (135°C).
2. In a medium size bowl, beat butter until light and fluffy; beat in 2 tablespoons of sugar, egg yolk, vanilla and almonds. Gradually add flour, beating to blend.
3. Pinch off pieces of dough the size of large walnuts and roll between your palms into round balls. Place 1½ inches apart on ungreased baking sheets; flatten each ball slightly.
4. Bake about 45 minutes until lightly browned. Cool on baking sheets until lukewarm.
5. Sift half of remaining powdered sugar onto a sheet of wax paper. Roll each cookie gently in the sugar. With fingers, pack more sugar over the cookies to depth of ⅛-inch. Place cookies on wire racks over wax paper and dust generously with more powdered sugar; let cool completely. May be stored up to 3 days in airtight container between sheets of wax paper.

Makes 36 cookies.

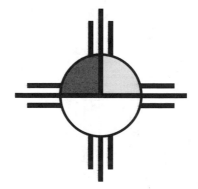

Piñon Nut Cookies

Always store piñon nuts in the refrigerator. They are high fat and become rancid quickly. The piñon tree grows well in New Mexico, but the nut crop is very erratic. Difficult to shell, these nuts are expensive but their taste is wonderful.

½ cup butter, softened
2 tablespoons powdered sugar
2 teaspoons grated orange peel
1 teaspoon vanilla extract
1 cup all-purpose flour
1 cup piñon nuts, finely chopped
½ teaspoon anise seed, crushed
⅛ teaspoon salt
2 cups powdered sugar

1. Preheat oven to 275ºF (135ºC).
2. In a medium bowl, beat butter, 2 tablespoons powdered sugar, orange peel and vanilla until creamy.
3. Stir in flour, nuts, anise seed and salt; mix well. Shape spoonfuls of dough into 1-inch balls. Place balls on ungreased cookie sheet 1 inch apart, flattening slightly.
4. Bake 30 to 35 minutes until edges are light golden brown.
5. Roll warm cookies in powdered sugar; cool and roll in powdered sugar again.

Makes 48 cookies.

Candied Pecans

Every winter when the pecans are harvested, I fix these. If you are not careful, you too will find them addictive.

1 cup packed brown sugar
⅓ cup fresh orange juice
4 cups pecan halves

1. Preheat oven to 350ºF (175ºC). Butter a 15 x 10-inch baking pan. Make a foil sheet of equal size and coat with butter.
2. In a medium bowl, combine brown sugar and orange juice. Add pecans and toss to coat.
3. Spread pecans on buttered pan. Bake for 10 to 12 minutes or until bubbly and golden brown, stirring occasionally.
4. Immediately spread pecans on buttered foil. Cool and break apart.

Makes 2 cups.

Cracker Toffee

The Chaves County Extension Service gave this recipe to my wife several years ago, and you have to try this easy-to-prepare treat. It is so simple to make and really does taste like real toffee.

1 package of saltine crackers
1 cup butter
1 cup firmly packed brown sugar
12 ounces semisweet chocolate morsels
½ cup crushed or chopped pecans

1. Preheat oven to 400ºF (205ºC). Line a square baking sheet with aluminum foil and spray with cooking spray
2. Lay saltines, side by side, on foil. Cover entire foil.
3. In a saucepan, bring butter and sugar to a boil, then pour mixture evenly over the saltines, covering surface. Bake for 5 to 6 minutes in oven.
4. Remove from oven and immediately sprinkle with chocolate morsels. When chocolate is soft, spread with spatula to make a smooth coating. Sprinkle pecans over top.
5. Cool in refrigerator and cut into bars.

Serves 6 or 8, depending on size of bars.

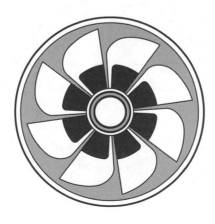

Mexican Orange Candy

What would Christmas be without candy? This orange treat is traditionally prepared in many New Mexico homes for the holiday celebrations.

3 cups sugar, divided
¼ cup boiling water
1 cup evaporated milk
dash of salt
2 teaspoons grated orange rind
1 cup pecans, coarsely chopped

1. In a saucepan, heat 1 cup sugar, stirring constantly until it caramelizes. When the sugar is golden brown add boiling water. Cook, stirring constantly, until it becomes a smooth syrup.
2. Add remaining sugar, milk and salt. Cook until soft ball stage, or 240ºF (120ºC), stirring constantly. Add orange peel; cool and stir in the nuts. When candy is at room temperature, beat till crystalline. Drop from a teaspoon onto waxed paper. Refrigerate until firm.

Makes 18 pieces.

New Mexico Pralines

After the Civil War, Confederate soldiers who came West brought their recipes for pralines, and they have been a part of our sweets ever since.

1 cup sugar
½ cup packed brown sugar
1 tablespoon corn syrup
3 tablespoons butter
½ cup milk
2 cups pecan halves
½ teaspoon vanilla extract

1. In a 2-quart saucepan over low heat, combine all ingredients except pecans and vanilla. Stir about 2 minutes. When mixture comes to a boil, cover and boil gently 3 minutes.
2. Uncover and insert a candy thermometer; continue cooking slowly until soft ball stage 240ºF (116ºC).
3. Remove the pan from heat and let sit undisturbed until temperature drops to 175ºF (80ºC). Remove thermometer, stir in the pecans and vanilla. Drop batter by tablespoonfuls onto waxed paper. Cool.

Makes about 1 dozen pralines.

New Mexico is becoming a major producer of pecans. This native American nut is a member of the hickory family. Care should be taken in storing them because of their high fat content. Refrigerate or freeze in airtight containers. Use them in both sweet and savory dishes.

Valencia Peanut Patties

Peanut fans will love these. They are easy to make.

2½ cups sugar
1 cup milk
⅔ cup white corn syrup
¼ teaspoon salt
1½ cups raw Valencia peanuts
1 tablespoon butter or margarine
1 teaspoon vanilla extract

1. Butter 12-cup muffin pan.
2. In saucepan, mix together sugar, milk and corn syrup. Stirring constantly, boil until sugar is dissolved.
3. Add salt and peanuts; cook, stirring occasionally, until firm ball stage 246ºF (120ºC). Remove from heat; add vanilla and butter. Beat until mixture starts to thicken. Drop rapidly into 12-cup muffin pan, dividing equally. Let stand and refrigerate until set.

Makes 12 patties.

Roosevelt County in New Mexico grows 90% of the Valencia peanuts in the nation. Each fall, they hold the Peanut Valley Festival. This celebration includes a peanut food fair, peanut Olympics and a juried peanut art show. For information call (505) 562-2631.

APPENDIX

GLOSSARY

Anaheim chiles
See New Mexico 6 chiles.

Anasazi beans
One of the most popular of the modern boutique beans, the Anasazi bean is also called the Aztec bean, Cave bean, New Mexico Appaloosa and sometimes Jacob's Cattle. This attractive purple-red and white bean cooks in about ⅔ the time of an ordinary pinto bean to a creamy even pink color. It has a sweet mild full flavor and a mealy texture, perfect for any New Mexico recipe.

ancho chiles
Ancho chiles are ripened and dried poblano chiles. These are the most popular dried chiles in Mexico. They vary from sweet to moderate heat.

anise seeds
Sweet and aromatic, these small elongated seeds taste like licorice. Anise seeds are used whole or crushed in a variety of foods including baked goods, stews, cheese, pickles, fish and shellfish.

avocado
Although many believe the avocado to be a vegetable, it is actually a fruit. It has a leathery skin and a soft, buttery flesh that yields to light pressure when ripe. Hard avocados will ripen if left on the counter for a few days. Haas avocados (California type) are smaller and darker than the emerald colored fruits grown in Florida. To keep avocados from discoloring after peeling, brush or sprinkle them with lemon juice. Even then, they should be peeled as close to serving time as possible.

Baco Noir

Baco Noir is a hybrid red wine with distinguished character and a flavor as powerful as Cabernet Sauvignon. It goes well with hearty meals such as barbecued ribs.

beans, dried

A Western staple, dried beans keep almost indefinitely. Before cooking, rinse beans well and sort through them, tossing out any small stones or other matter. Some beans require soaking prior to cooking. Cook beans slowly on the stove top in a crockpot or in a pressure cooker. Cooking times vary depending on the variety of bean. Properly prepared, cooked beans are tender but still firm. When you are short of time or only need a small amount of beans, you will find canned varieties useful, although they are sometimes mushy.

bell peppers

Bell peppers are the only member of the genus *capsicum* to lack capsaicin; hence they lack the hotness of taste and are comparatively "sweet." They can be green, red, yellow, orange and, more rarely, white, purple and brown. Until recently, bell peppers of any color other than green were rarely available. The green pepper is actually an immature red pepper. Bell peppers become sweeter as they ripen, with the green slightly bitter and the red and yellow the sweetest. Bell peppers, particularly the red ones, are an excellent source of both vitamin C and beta carotene.

Big Jim chiles

Big Jim chiles are available in mild, medium hot and hot varieties and are the most commonly available fresh (and freshly roasted) chiles in New Mexico and the Southwest.

black beans (*frijoles negros,* turtle beans)

These small dark beans have a hearty flavor. They are often used in South American cooking, and their very dark purple-blue color makes them attractive in salsas.

black pepper

Peppercorns (*piper nigrum*) came to the Western world originally from Madagascar. The success of medieval spice traders made black pepper more widely available, and now ground pepper is one of the most

common spices in European and American cuisine; it is found on nearly every dinner table in many parts of the world. Pepper looses its potency quickly after being ground; for best results, buy peppercorns and a small pepper mill, grinding only what you need.

black-eyed peas (cowpeas)
These are the seeds of the cowpea, an annual vine. Their tan coloring with black spots gives them the name "black-eyed." According to legend, black-eyed peas are supposed to provide good luck when consumed on New Year's Day.

Cabernet Sauvignon
With its primary flavor being black currant with classic cassis and cedar characteristics, this dark red wine, known for its high levels of extract and tannin, is often blended with complementary varieties, like Merlot. Cabernet Sauvignon complements red meats, hearty red pastas, strong-flavored cheeses and dark chocolate.

cascabel chiles
Fresh cascabel chiles are round, about 1½ inches in diameter. They are quite hot and have a distinctive flavor; drying them gives them a nutty taste.

cayenne pepper, cayenne chiles
Cayenne chiles are extremely hot, small, narrow red peppers. Ground red pepper is made from ground dried cayenne chiles and is often called cayenne pepper. The name originally came from the city of Cayenne, in French Guiana. Cayenne is usually used in its ground form, although some types of cooking (for example, Szechuan) do use whole chiles. Cayenne also has been used for centuries for its medicinal properties, most notably for gastrointestinal and circulatory problems.

Chardonnay
Depending on where the grapes are grown and how they are fermented, the flavor of this very popular wine can range from semi-sweet to sour and from heady to light, with hints of apple, tangerine, lemon, lime, melon and oak. Grown in the cooler winemaking regions of New Mexico, the Chardonnay grape is also an important component in champagne. Chardonnay goes well with poultry dishes, light red meat dishes and rich creamy sauces.

cheddar cheese
Cheddar cheese is a firm cheese made from cow's milk. It originated in the English village of Cheddar in Somerset and becomes sharper with age. Cheddar cheese is available in several varieties, including mild, medium, sharp, New York Style, Colby/longhorn, white and Vermont. In recipes calling for cheddar cheese, you can use any variety and will probably get the best results using the one you prefer.

cheese
Cheese is nutritious dairy food made from the milk of cows, sheep, goats and other mammals. There are hundreds of types of cheese produced all over the world. Cheddar and Monterey Jack are the most commonly used cheeses in Southwestern cooking.

Chenin Blanc
Wines produced from this excellent white grape can vary from fresh, lively and fruity-light to dry, fine, full and aggressive. This wine complements poultry or pork dishes.

chevre cheese
Chevre cheese is pure white goat cheese. With a delightfully tart flavor that easily distinguishes it from other cheeses, chevre cheese can range in texture from moist and creamy to dry and semi-firm. It comes in a variety of shapes and takes on a sour taste when it is old. After opening, always wrap it tightly and store in the refrigerator.

chickpeas
See garbanzo beans.

chile peppers
Chile peppers are vegetables of the pod-bearing *capsicum* family. There are hundreds of varieties of chiles, and new strains are being developed frequently. Whether whole, dry, crushed or powdered, they are the heart and soul of New Mexico cuisine. Fresh, they are considered a vegetable, not just a spice. Fresh chile is seasonally available, but frozen, canned and dried are available year round.

chile powder
Pure chile powder is made from finely ground dried chiles. It is usually made from red chiles and comes in a variety of flavors and heat levels.

chili powder

Chili powder is a spice mix usually consisting of chile powder and other spices and herbs, including cumin, garlic and oregano.

chipotle chiles

Chipotle chiles are smoked and dried jalapeños with a very wrinkly brown appearance. They have a unique smoky taste and are very hot.

chocolate

The first use of chocolate has been credited to the Mayan and Aztec cultures, who used the beans of the cocoa (*cacao*) tree as a form of currency and as a bitter ceremonial drink after the beans were crushed into a paste. Spanish explorers brought some back to Europe from the New World, and eventually its use spread, at first only for the elite who could afford it. The Europeans sweetened the chocolate with sugar and its popularity grew. Eventually the Industrial Revolution made it readily available to everyone. European and American chocolate is sweetened with sugar, while Mexican chocolate frequently contains cinnamon, vanilla, cloves and ground almonds as well as sugar.

chorizo

Chorizo is a spicy, highly flavorful sausage usually made from pork (or pork and beef), chile, garlic and other spices. It is available both in links and in bulk and is most commonly used with eggs and other breakfast recipes.

cilantro

Cilantro (Mexican parsley, Chinese parsley, fresh coriander) is actually the name for the leaves of the coriander plant. These leaves are similar in appearance to flat-leaf parsley but have a completely different flavor, with a citrusy biting tang that people seem to either love or hate. Cilantro adds its distinctive flavor to many dishes and is often used as a garnish. To keep it fresh, store it in the refrigerator with the stems in water and plastic loosely covering the leafy tops.

cinnamon

Cinnamon is a spice derived from the bark of the cinnamon tree, a small evergreen originally native to southern India and Ceylon (Sri Lanka). It is sold in sticks (actually tightly wound quills) or ground as a powder. In

addition to all kinds of dishes from sweet-savory to sweet, cinnamon is used for medicinal purposes, and cinnamon oil is even used as an insecticide.

coriander

Coriander is an annual herb of the parsley family. Its leaves are referred to as cilantro. As a spice, the word "coriander" refers to the seeds (or small fruits), which have a dusky citrus flavor and are often associated with Eastern cooking. Coriander can be purchased ground or as whole dried seeds.

cornhusks

When corn is harvested, the husks are removed and dried. In food preparation, all silk is removed from the husks, which are then softened by soaking and are used to wrap food before it is cooked, making a natural jacket to hold food together while steaming. Several small corn husks may be overlapped to make larger wrappings, as in tamale preparation.

cornmeal

Cornmeal is a staple in Southwestern kitchens. It comes coarsely or finely ground in yellow, white and blue. The colors refer to the corn—yellow, white or blue corn. Each type has a slightly different flavor and consistency. Most recipes calling for cornmeal refer to the yellow variety unless specified differently. In general, the white is more delicate while the blue has a stronger flavor and tougher texture.

cottage cheese

Cottage cheese is made from separating milk or cream into curds and whey. The result is a soft, spoonable cheese that is white and mild but faintly sour in taste. It is often made from low-fat or skim milk.

cowpeas

See black-eyed peas.

cream cheese

Cream cheese is a mildly tangy, smooth, creamy-textured spreadable cheese. Developed in 1872, this soft cheese is made from cow's milk. Neufchatel cheese can be used in place of cream cheese for a lower butterfat content.

cumin

Originally cultivated in Persia (Iran) and the Mediterranean region, cumin has been used as an aromatic spice since the days of the Old Testament. This powerful, sometimes dominating spice can be used to season many dishes, as it draws out their natural sweetness. It is traditionally added to Middle-Eastern, Indian, Cuban and Mexican-style foods. It is frequently found in commercially produced chili powder and curry powder. Recipes may call for whole cumin seed or for ground cumin.

French Colombard

Because of its high-acid juice, this grape is used in making semi-sweet white wines and champagnes, and it is a principal white wine grape in the Mesilla Valley. French Colombard goes well with appetizers, Monterey Jack cheese or chicken, and it can be served as a dessert wine.

French-American Hybrid wines

Northern New Mexico is well suited to the growing of these varieties. Both reds and whites generally tend to be soft and especially pleasant to drink young.

frijoles

See pinto beans.

garbanzo beans (chickpeas)

These rounded, beige-colored beans have a nutty flavor and a buttery texture and are often used in salads. They are also a noted ingredient in many types of Middle Eastern and Indian cuisine such as hummus and falafel.

habanero chiles

These lantern-shaped chiles have a fruity flavor and are the hottest of all chiles.

hominy

Hominy consists of yellow or white corn that has been soaked in lime to remove its germ and hard outer hull, a process dating back 10,000 years in Central American cultures. Now available dried, frozen or canned, hominy is an important ingredient of many popular Mexican and Southwestern recipes, including posole and menudo. In the Southeastern part of the United States, hominy is pressed into patties and fried or ground into small grains called hominy grits.

jalapeño chiles

These popular chiles have a good amount of heat—ranging from hot to very hot—and rich flavor. They are about three inches long and usually feature rounded tips—the sharper the tips the hotter the chile. The red ones have a much richer, warmer flavor than the green ones. Try to find fresh jalapeños; canned ones aren't as fiery or as tasty. When smoked and dried they are called chipotle chiles.

jicama

Also called the Mexican potato or Mexican turnip, the jicama is a brown-skinned root vegetable that looks like a turnip but has a very mild sweet and starchy flavor. To use, remove the peel, including the fibrous flesh directly under the skin. Cut or slice and serve in salads and salsas. You can also sauté it and use it in stir fries; it stays crisp when cooked, similar to water chestnuts. Unlike turnip greens, the leaves of the jicama are inedible.

juniper berries

Juniper berries are actually tiny cones of an evergreen shrub, the juniper. These blue-green berries are used in northern European and Scandinavian cooking to enhance the flavor of meats and wild game; they also give gin its distinctive flavor. In herbal medicine, they have a variety of medicinal purposes including treating urinary tract infections.

lard

Lard is a soft white solid or semi-solid animal fat produced from rendered pig fat. Until recent years, when it was deemed to be unhealthy compared to vegetable fats, lard was one of the most frequently used ingredients in traditional New Mexican cooking. Certain items such as pie crusts, tortillas, sopapillas and biscochitos simply do not have the traditional taste or texture when another fat is substituted for lard. Because of its reputation, freshly rendered lard is rarely available and the processed flavorless blocks in your supermarket are of little value. I have used vegetable oil in most recipes. If you have fresh lard available, by all means use it. There is no substitute for the taste it offers. It should be noted that lard, for all its reputation, has approximately half the cholesterol of butter and no trans fat.

mango

Once known as the "food of the Gods" in Southern and Southeast Asia, the mango is one of the most popular fruits in Mexico and growing in popularity in New Mexico. It has a very sweet peach-like taste and flowery aroma. The flesh is juicy and deep yellow. To slice the fruit, free it from the pit in large pieces. The large fruit trees grow in tropical and subtropical climates throughout the world. Mango is especially delicious in salsa.

masa

Masa literally means "dough" in Spanish, although it is generally understood to mean "corn dough." It is made from dried corn kernels that have been softened in a lime (calcium hydroxide) solution, then ground. Fresh frozen masa is sometimes available in your supermarket. Masa harina is dried, powdered masa. It is readily available and can be used in any recipe that calls for masa.

Merlot

A premium red wine grape, Merlot has a softer, more delicate character and less tannin than the Cabernet Sauvignon, and its flavor hints of plum, black cherry, violet and orange. It is excellent served with wild fowl, beef and other heavy dishes as well as Camembert cheese and chocolate.

mole

Mole is the Spanish word for "mixture" or "concoction." Dozens of different mole sauces, quite unlike each other, are used in contemporary Mexico. In New Mexico, the mole sauce usually indicated is the one with the more complete name "mole poblano." This dark brown sauce is created with a mixture of dried chile peppers (usually ancho, pasilla, mulatto, poblano and/or chipotle), nuts, spices, various other ingredients and unsweetened chocolate, which gives the sauce its unique taste. Incidentally, the final "e" is pronounced, unlike the name of the digging animal, the mole.

Monterey Jack cheese

Made from cow's milk and developed by Franciscan monks in Monterey, California, Monterey Jack cheese has a buttery, bland taste and melts easily, making it a favorite for hot sandwiches and various recipes. An aged version of this cheese, known as Dry Jack, is harder and can be grated.

mozzarella cheese
Mozzarella cheese is a white cheese made from either whole or partially skimmed cow's milk. It has a firm texture and is usually available in sliced, small round or shredded form. The "low moisture" varieties may have preservatives added.

Muscat
Scores of different spicy Muscat grapes are cultivated in southern New Mexico and range in sweetness. Some are primarily dessert wines, while others go well with cheese, apples and pears.

New Mexico 6 (formerly Anaheim) chiles
The mildest variety of chile, these taste pretty much like bell peppers with a bit of a bite.

New Mexico chiles
New Mexico chiles are relatively slim and range in length from five to eight inches and in color from light green to deep red. There are two main varieties of New Mexico chiles—New Mexico 6 (formerly Anaheim) and Big Jim, which vary from mild to hot.

nonreactive cookware
Certain metals, especially aluminum, react with the acids in chiles and tomatoes. These acids can actually leach the metal away and into the foods and can affect color and flavor as well. Do not store processed chiles or tomatoes in aluminum containers. Uncoated copper and cast iron cookware are also reactive. Nonreactive cookware is made from clay, coated copper (unscratched), enamel, glass, plastic or stainless steel. Aluminum pans with a Teflon or other protective coating are considered nonreactive as long as they are not scratched.

nuts
Nuts are important flavoring agents in Southwestern cooking and are sometimes ground and stirred into sauces as a thickening agent, adding flavor and body. Toasted nuts are often used as a garnish or in baking. Pecans, peanuts, and piñon (pine) nuts are popular nuts in New Mexico.

nuts, ground
Ground nuts are often called for in Southwestern recipes. To grind nuts, place ⅓ to ½ cup at a time in the work bowl of a food processor or

blender. Process them in short pulses just until ground. Too much grinding will give you nut butter.

nuts, toasted
Toasting nuts enhances their flavor. To toast nuts, spread them in a single layer on an ungreased pan or cookie sheet; bake at 350°F (175°C), stirring occasionally until they are done. Nuts are toasted when they are lightly browned. Almonds, pecans and walnuts take 7 to 12 minutes. Pine nuts toast more rapidly, in 5 to 7 minutes.

papaya
The papaya is a nearly oval fruit with a creamy golden yellow skin, orange-yellow flesh and scores of shiny black seeds conveniently packed in its center. The flavor is sweet and somewhat similar to that of a cantaloupe; in some types it tastes quite musky. When slightly underripe, the flesh is firm (perfect for making into relishes and salsas); when ripe, it is soft and very juicy. Rich in vitamin C, the papaya contains the enzyme papain, useful in tenderizing meat and as an ingredient in herbal supplements for digestive and other problems. Originally native to southern Mexico and Central America, the papaya now grows in all tropical and subtropical countries.

parmesan cheese
Parmesan cheese is a hard, dry cheese made from skim cow's milk. It has a rich, sharp flavor and is usually graded or shredded for use, particularly in Italian cooking.

pasilla chiles
These thin, red-brown chiles have a dusty, raisin-like taste and are of medium heat.

pecans
The state tree of Texas, the pecan is a species of hickory tree native to the southern United States. Commercial growing of pecans has expanded greatly in Southern New Mexico in recent years. This oil-rich nut has a buttery flavor and is eaten fresh or in salads, desserts and candies.

pepper
Pepper comes in many forms, all in the genus *capsicum*, including chile, black pepper (peppercorn), bell pepper, cayenne pepper, paprika and

pimento. All peppers except the bell pepper include the chemical capsaicin, with makes them hot or bitter to the taste and dissuades mammals from eating them. Capsaicin is also used in medicine as a topical pain reliever for arthritis and other conditions.

picante sauce
Picante sauce is similar to salsa but usually more pureed. Picante is a Spanish adjective that derives from picar, which means "to sting." The term is often used interchangeably with the term "salsa."

pico de gallo
Salsa cruda ("raw sauce"), also known as pico de gallo ("cock's beak"), *salsa mexicana* ("Mexican sauce") or *salsa fresca* ("fresh sauce"), is made with raw tomatoes, lime juice, chili peppers, onions, cilantro leaves and other coarsely chopped raw ingredients. It is used as a condiment similar to salsa and is commonly served with tacos and fajitas.

piñon nuts
Piñon nuts are the seeds of the piñon (*Pinus edulis*) pine, a two-needled scrubby evergreen that grows wild in New Mexico, Colorado, Arizona and Utah between 5,000 and 8,000 feet in elevation. The piñon is the state tree of New Mexico, and the local Indians have been consuming the nuts for centuries. Raw or toasted, they are delicious by themselves, or they can be enjoyed as an ingredient in or sprinkled on a variety of dishes, salads and desserts. Store them tightly covered in the refrigerator or freezer, depending on how quickly they are to be used.

pinto beans (*frijoles*)
These attractive brown-speckled beans have a pale or pinkish background when dry. Cooking changes them to a dull pink or grey-brown. A staple of Southwestern cooking, pinto beans are what you will usually find on your plate in restaurants, whether by the side of enchiladas or wrapped in a burrito.

poblano chiles
Poblano chiles are heart-shaped, more like a bell pepper, and a little darker colored and somewhat sweeter and hotter than the New Mexico Big Jims. They are the chiles most frequently used for chiles rellenos.

pumpkin seeds

Pumpkin seeds with the shells or husks removed are also known as *pepitas*. These seeds, with their sweet and nutty flavor and a malleable chewy texture, are quite nutritious. Store them in a cool, dry place. To toast pumpkin seeds, spread them in a single layer on an ungreased pan or cookie sheet. Bake at 350ºF (175ºC) 13 to 15 minutes, stirring and checking frequently. Although they are available year round, they are freshest in the fall when pumpkins are in season.

queso

Queso is the Spanish word for cheese.

red pepper

See cayenne pepper.

red pepper flakes

Red pepper flakes, or crushed red peppers, are just what their name suggests, flaked dried ripe chiles. Most chile flake mixtures are quite hot.

red pepper sauce

Red pepper sauce is a commercially bottled condiment made from vinegar, spices and hot chiles. It adds heat but little in the way of flavor. Many restaurants place small bottles on the table for patrons who want to give their meals a bit of an extra kick. Some cooks keep it on hand for the same reason.

rice

Rice exists in a large number of varieties, but Mexican cooking usually calls for long- or medium-grain white rice. Other types of rice, such as brown or basmati, may be used, but cooking times will need to be adjusted and the flavor and consistency of the rice will be different. Southwestern dishes sometimes use wild rice, which really isn't rice. It is the seed of an aquatic grass once harvested only by Native Americans who lived by the Great Lakes. It makes a popular side dish, particularly with game.

ricotta cheese

This Italian cheese is a by-product from the production of mozzarella and other cheeses. It is similar to cottage cheese in texture, although lighter, sweeter and smoother. Ricotta cheese is a key ingredient in cheesecake and lasagna.

Riesling
Also known as White Riesling, this grape produces some of New Mexico's most popular wines, with a variety of sweetness depending on time of harvest. Aromas and flavors of apricots and melons characterize its bouquet. Riesling is excellent for dinner, accompanying seafood or poultry as well as cheese and fruit. It can also be served with dessert.

ristras
Ristras are ropes of dried red chile often used for decoration. Chile pods in ristras can be reconstituted into a red chile puree.

Ruby Cabernet
This grape has a powerful, astringent flavor, variously described as green olive, weedy and tannic. After being aged and bottled, it gradually loses its astringent taste and develops a fruity bouquet. Ruby Cabernet is an excellent wine to complement beef or spicy foods.

salsa
A spicy sauce of chopped, usually uncooked fruit and/or vegetables, including tomatoes, onions and chile peppers. Salsa has surpassed ketchup, becoming America's number one condiment.

salsa verde
Salsa verde is a cooked Mexican green salsa usually made with tomatillos, hot green peppers, garlic, onion and salt.

Sauvignon Blanc
Also known as Fume Blanc, this white wine grape has adapted well to New Mexico's climate and soils. It produces a distinctive, grassy, herbaceous in character, dry white wine. Sauvignon Blanc is an excellent table wine to serve with seafood, fowl or vegetarian dishes.

serrano chiles
Hotter than jalapeños, these chiles are usually shorter and thinner and are a mainstay in salsas.

Seyval Blanc
The most popular French hybrid white wine is Seyval Blanc. This delicately flavored wine goes well with poultry (especially turkey) and lighter seafood entrees.

squash blossoms

Squash blossoms from pumpkins are preferred for use in Southwestern cooking because they are larger than those from zucchini, but either can be used. They are extremely perishable and are best used the day they are bought.

tequila

Tequila is a pale, sharp-tasting liquor distilled from the blue agave plant, which thrives in arid, hot climates like the central plains of Northern Mexico. The liquor is named after the town of Tequila, located in the state of Jalisco, where production started more than 200 years ago. Tequila is a main component of the popular Mexican drink, the margarita. There are many different varieties of tequila and many different types of margaritas.

tomatillo

Tomatillos are fat little vegetables the size of robust cherry tomatoes. They grow in papery husks reminiscent of Japanese lanterns and taste best when they are brilliant green in color. By the time they begin to turn yellow, they have lost some of their acid freshness. This happens when they are lightly cooked too, but then they develop a gentler flavor and become more luscious. Uncooked, chopped tomatillos are the basis for chunky green salsas. Select tomatillos with their husks still drawn tightly around them. Husk and rinse off the sticky residue before using them.

tomato

The tomato, a plant native to South America, is widely cultivated for its edible, fleshy, usually red fruit. Roasting tomatoes gives them a faintly mysterious flavor. This works best with truly ripe, red tomatoes. To roast and peel tomatoes, set the oven control to broil. Arrange cored tomatoes with their top surfaces about 5 inches from the heat. Broil, turning occasionally, until the skin is blistered and evenly browned, about 5 to 8 minutes. The skins will be easy to remove. If the tomatoes are roasted on aluminum foil, the cleanup will be easy and you'll be able to save any juice they give off as they roast.

tortilla

Tortillas are round, flat unleavened breads made from ground wheat or corn. They are the basis of Mexican cookery. Tortillas are rolled, folded, used as dippers, fried crisp and munched fresh. Corn tortillas can be cut

into wedges and fried for chips. For the best chips, fry tortillas that are at least one day old. Flour tortillas, softer than those made from corn, are becoming more popular in New Mexico. Commercially made tortillas of both kinds are best stored in the freezer until needed. To soften tortillas, warm them on a hot ungreased skillet or griddle for about 30 seconds to 1 minute. They can also be warmed in a 250°F (120°C) degree oven for 15 minutes. Or, wrap several in dampened microwavable paper toweling or microwave plastic wrap and microwave on HIGH (100% power) for 15 to 20 seconds. To keep warmed tortillas soft, place in tortilla holder or plastic bag.

tripe
Tripe usually means the linings of pig and sheep stomachs. Tripe is the identifying ingredient of traditional Menudo, a hearty soup. Tripe needs to be thoroughly rinsed in three or four changes of cold water before it can be used.

walnuts
Walnuts are a delicious complement to a variety of recipes.

Zinfandel
Zinfandel grapes produce a variety of wines from deep red to a pale rose to white. The red skins give the wine a robust flavor and color. When the skins are removed, the wine becomes pale or white, light and sweet. White Zinfandel goes well with cream sauces, fish, pork and other lighter meals, including Asian and Latin foods. Red Zinfandel is hearty enough to match up with beef, lamb, spicy foods and thick red sauces. All Zinfandels pair well with different types of cheeses.

ALTITUDE ADJUSTMENTS

High-Altitude Baking

If you live at an altitude above 3,500 feet (most of New Mexico), you will find that you may need to make adjustments in many recipes to get desired results. These recipes were written for altitudes of 3,500 feet and under. Remember that every recipe is different, and any or all of these adjustments may be required. The suggestions here are only meant to be a rough guide—each recipe is different and you will need to experiment to see what actually works best for you. It will help if you keep notes of how you adjust recipes until you know what works best.

Because higher altitudes have lower air pressure, leavening agents (yeast, baking powder and baking soda) cause the gases in breads or cakes to expand faster, so baked goods rise faster (often over-rising then collapsing). One teaspoon of baking powder at 5,000 feet produces 20 percent more volume than at sea level. Bread also rises faster and must be watched.

The three basic adjustments for high-altitude baking are as follows:

1. Reduce baking powder.
For each teaspoon decrease:
⅛ teaspoon at 3,500 to 5,000 feet
⅛ to ¼ teaspoon at 5,000 to 6,000 feet
¼ teaspoon for 7,000 feet or higher

2. Reduce sugar.
For each cup decrease:
0 to 1 tablespoon at 3,500 to 5,000 feet
0 to 2 tablespoons at 5,000 to 6,000 feet
1 to 3 tablespoons for 7,000 feet or higher

3. Increase liquid.
For each cup add:
1 to 2 tablespoons at 3,500 to 5,000 feet
2 to 4 tablespoons at 5,000 to 6,000 feet
3 to 4 tablespoons for 7,000 feet or higher

Typically, all three of these adjustments are needed. Ingredients such as eggs or butter are considered liquids.

In addition to these changes, you should increase the baking temperature 15 to 25 degrees (unless using a glass pan) to help "set" the cell framework and prevent collapsing. You then may need to reduce the baking time by about 20 percent to prevent over baking.

Shortening can also be a problem. Too much fat in a batter will weaken the cell structure. The substitution of margarine for butter or shortening can noticeably affect the texture and produce an inferior taste. Solid shortening gives better results at this altitude because it holds more liquid.

Regarding eggs, higher egg content provides more protein for a better cell framework, so extra large eggs should be used. Without enough egg, the batter will be less stable and the final product will be too dry. Some cakes, especially angel food and sponge, require an even greater number of eggs. Also, eggs should be used at room temperature, and be careful not to over-beat them, as this adds too much air, aggravating the rapid-rising problem and the dryness.

Yeast bread

Most yeast bread recipes are reliable at most altitudes. However, since fermentation of sugar is faster at higher altitudes, breads rise much faster—in one-third the time noted for lower altitudes. Be careful that the dough does not rise more than double its bulk. Also, the faster rising time does not allow the flavor to fully develop. Punching down the dough twice instead of once will improve flavor as well as texture. Salt acts as a yeast retardant, so don't bake bread at high altitude without it. And don't use self-rising flour.

Another problem with breads at high altitudes is dryness. Decreasing the flour specified in the recipe just enough to make a stiff batter or soft dough that is handled easily (could be up to one-quarter less) will help make your bread less dry. Sifting flour can result in reduction of flour, and on a humid day could add some needed moisture. Whole wheat and "dark" flours require more liquid than white. Fresh fruits and vegetables add liquid to dough in the knead cycle. The more liquid (to a certain point) the more interesting, complex and varied the crumb and crust.

Bread machines represent another problem at altitude. To use the bake cycle in the machine, you must be very careful about the amount of additional liquid. Give up the "overnight" or time/delay mode. Gold Medal flour recommends using active dry yeast in lieu of bread-machine or Rapid Rise yeast. If the dough is coming out too dry, Fleischmann's recommends adding a couple teaspoons of water to the dough until it comes out in a tight, shiny ball. If the bread caves in on itself, reduce the yeast by ¼ to ½ teaspoon.

Quick breads

Quick breads have various textures from muffin-like to cake-like. If muffins seem dry, reduce sugar by at least one teaspoon. Also, be careful not to over-mix, as this causes peaked tops rather than the preferred rounded tops. If you note a bitter taste, try decreasing the baking soda or baking powder slightly. Usually, both shortening and sugar can be reduced by as much as one-fourth of the total amount and still provide tasty bread. For biscuits, try adding a tablespoon of milk to each cup of flour and reducing baking powder slightly.

Cookies

Most cookie recipes yield acceptable results at high altitude, but many can be improved by slightly increasing baking temperature. Cookies with lots of chocolate, nuts or fruit may need a reduction of baking powder/soda by up to half. Also, cookie recipes often contain a higher proportion of sugar and fat than necessary. Up to one-fourth of the sugar can be replaced with nonfat dry milk without loss in quality.

Pie crusts

To get a tender and flaky crust, it helps to have all ingredients at 70 degrees (room temperature) and preheat the oven. Handle the dough lightly and no more than absolutely necessary. Too much flour produces a tough crust; too little makes it soggy. Sometimes, adding more liquid (up to 25 percent more but not so much as to make the crust soggy) helps to hydrate the flour. Using a non-shiny, metal pan generally helps achieve a good, brown crust.

Cake mixes

Follow the high-altitude adjustments given on the mix box. These have been tested to work with the mix's specific ingredients. You may still need to make a few minor adjustments; adding an egg is what you can try first.

Other High Altitude Adjustments

The boiling point

The important point to know about cooking anything at higher altitudes is that when the atmospheric pressure is less, the temperature required for water to boil is less. What boils at 212°F at sea level will boil at 208°F at 2,000 feet, at 203°F at 5,000 feet, 198°F at 7,500 feet and 194°F at 10,000 feet. Cooking food in water boiling at these lower temperatures

takes longer, because the water is boiling at a lower temperature and thus the food is cooking at a lower temperature. For example, the "3-minute egg" will take more time. Also, a bowl of boiling soup is not as hot. The following are a few recommendations for specific types of cooking. Again, these are only meant as a guide; experiment and see what works best for you.

Candy making

To prevent excessive water evaporation while cooking, decrease your final cooking temperature by the difference in the boiling point of water for your altitude and that of sea level. This is an approximate decrease of 2°F for every increase of 1,000 feet in elevation. You may need to use a longer cooking time.

Deep-fat frying

The lower boiling point requires lowering the temperature of the fat to prevent food from over-cooking on the outside and under-cooking on the inside. The decrease varies with the recipe, but a rough guide is to lower the frying temperature about 3°F for every increase of 1,000 feet.

Puddings and cream pie fillings

Above 5,000 feet, the temperatures obtained with a double boiler are not high enough for maximum gelatinization of starch. Carefully use direct heat rather than a double boiler.

Miscellaneous other changes for altitude

In general, all stovetop and oven-baked foods (if the temperature is not adjusted) take longer at altitude. Pasta needs a hard boil and will take longer; check for doneness by taste not time. Dried beans need to be cooked as much as twice as long as at sea level; a pressure cooker is a great help here. Slow stews need about one hour extra for every 1,000 feet above 4,000 feet. Baked items usually need higher cooking temperatures (which sometimes leads to shorter cooking times) and sometimes light covering with foil to help hold in moisture. Cooking bags are great for turkeys and roasts (follow directions that come with the bags and use a meat thermometer to ensure doneness). Experiment and find out what works best for you.

WHERE TO BUY CHILES

The chile products used in these recipes are widely available in supermarkets and specialty stores in major metropolitan areas around the country. If you have difficulty finding chiles in your locality, call one of these reliable sources. Many of them provide regular mail-order services. You can order from a number of them off the Internet, and some of these can even overnight you fresh or frozen green chile in season.

SOUTHWEST

Apple Canyon Gourmet
P.O. Box 16494
Albuquerque, NM 87191
505 332 2000
1-800-992-4659
www.applecanyon.com

Bueno Foods
2001 4th Street SW
Albuquerque, NM 87102
505-243-2722
1-800-95CHILE
www.buenofoods.com

Casados Farms
Box 852
San Juan Pueblo, NM 87566
505-852-2433

Chile Addict
325 Eubank NE
Albuquerque, NM 87123
505-237-9070
www.chileaddictstore.com

The Chile Shop
109 East Water Street
Santa Fe, NM 87501
505-983-6080
www.thechileshop.com

Chile Traditions
8204 Montgomery Blvd. NE
Albuquerque, NM 87109
505-888-3166
1 877 VERY HOT
www.chiletraditions.com

Los Chileros
401 2nd. St. S.W.
Albuquerque, NM 87102
505-768-1100
1-888-328-2445
www.888eatchile.com

Da Gift Basket
P.O. Box 2085
Los Lunas, NM 87031
505-865-3645
1-877-468-2444
www.dagiftbasket.com

Graves Farm & Garden
6265 Graves Road
Roswell, NM 88203
575-622-1889
rgraves@dfn.com

Hatch Chile Express
P.O. Box 350
Hatch, NM 87937
575-267-3226
1-800-292-4454
www.hatch-chile.com

Hobson Gardens
3656 Hobson Road
Roswell, NM 88203
575-622-7289
Seasonal operation

Jane Butel's Pecos Valley Spice Co.
2655 Pan American NE, Suite F
Albuquerque, NM 87017
505-243-2622
www.pecosvalley.com

NM Chili.Com
2315 Hendola NE
Albuquerque, NM 87110
505-217-2105
1-888-336-4228
www.nmchili.com
wholesale:
www.wholesalechili.com

Pendery's
1221 Manufacturing Street
Dallas, Texas 75207
1-800-533-1870
www.penderys.com

Santa Fe Chile Co.
    See Apple Canyon Gourmet

Santa Fe School of Cooking
116 West San Francisco Street
Santa Fe, NM 87501
505-983-4511
1-800-982-4688
www.santafeschoolofcooking.com

WEST & NORTHWEST
La Palma
2884 Twenty-Fourth Street
San Francisco, CA 94110
415-647-1500
fax: 415-647-1710

EAST
The Hot Shoppe
311 S. Clinton St.
Syracuse NY 13202
1-888-468-3287 (HOTEATS)
www.hotshoppe.com

Mo Hotta–Mo Betta
P.O. Box 1026
Savannah, GA 31402
1-800-462-3220
www.mohotta.com

WHERE TO BUY NEW MEXICO WINES

Most of New Mexico's wineries are small to medium-sized operations. You can visit with the winemakers, who will be happy to let you sample their wines. Visiting these wineries or purchasing their wines at your local store gives you the flavor of New Mexico like nothing else. The New Mexico Vine and Wine Society (http://www.vineandwine.org/) and the New Mexico Wine Growers Association (http://www.nmwine.com/) are the two groups who promote the wines of New Mexico. A free detailed map showing the location of wineries in the Land of Enchantment is available free by writing to New Mexico Wine Growers Association, P.O. Box 3511, Santa Fe, New Mexico 87504. You can also find New Mexico wineries and maps showing their locations (as well as humorous descriptions of the wines) at http://wine.appellationamerica.com/wine region/New-Mexico.html. Listed below is detailed information about New Mexico wineries, including web sites and contact information. For a good introduction to various types of wine, including serving suggestions, see www.wineintro.com.

One other piece of information to keep in mind is that it is still illegal to ship wine to some states; in fact, it as actually a felony in a few. To see if wine can be shipped to your state, see www.wineintro.com/basics/shipping. Shipping in and out of New Mexico is not a problem; you need to see if wine can be shipped INTO your state. Here is a list of New Mexico wineries that offer fine wines.

Anasazi Fields, Inc.
26 Camino de los Pueblitos
Placitas, NM 87043
505-867-3062
anasazifieldswinery@att.net
www.anasazifieldswinery.com

Anderson Valley Vineyards
4920 Rio Grande Blvd. NW
Albuquerque, NM 87107
505-344-7266

Arena Blanca Winery
7320 U.S. Hwy 54/70 North
Alamogordo, NM 88301
575-437-0602, or
800-368-3081
www.pistachiotreeranch.com

Balagna Winery
223 Rio Bravo Drive
Los Alamos, NM 87544
Phone: 505-672-3678
Fax: 505-672-1482

Bees Brothers Winery
(Specializes in Mead)
619 Nowicki Lane
Albuquerque, NM 87105
Phone: 505-452-3191 message
Fax: 505-452-3192
www.beesbrothers.com

Black Mesa Winery
1502 State Highway 68
Box 308
Velarde, NM 87582
505-852-2820
Phone & Fax: 1-800-852-6372
www.blackmesawinery.com

Blue Teal Winery
    See Southwest Wines
www.blueteal.com

Casa Rondeña Winery
733 Chavez Road NW
Los Ranchos de Albuquerque
NM 87107
505-344-5911
505-343-1823
800-706-1699
www.casarondena.com

Chateau Sassenage
901 Caballo Rd.
P.O. Box 1606
Truth or Consequences, NM 87901
575-894-7244

Corrales Winery
6275 Corrales Road
Corrales, NM 87048
505-898-5165
www.corraleswinery.com

Domaine Cheurlin
500 Main Street
Truth or Consequences, NM 87901
575-894-0837

Duvallay Vineyards
500 Main Street
Truth or Consequences, NM 87901
Office: 575-894-7122
Winery: 575-894-3226

Gruet Winery
8400 Pan American Frwy NE
Albuquerque, NM 87113
505-821-0055
888-857-WINE (9463)
Fax: 505-857-0066
www.gruetwinery.com

Heart of the Desert Vineyard
& Tasting Room
Eagle Ranch
7288 Hwy 54/70
Alamogordo, NM 88310
575-434-0035
800-432-0999
Fax: 575-434-2132
www.eagleranchpistachios.com

Jacona Valley Vineyard
311 County Road 84
Santa Fe, NM 87506
505 660 7241

La Chiripada Winery
Hwy. 75
PO Box 191
Dixon, NM 87527
505-579-4437
800-528-7801
www.lachiripada.com

La Querencia Vineyards & Winery
980 Bosque Farms Blvd.
Bosque Farms, NM   87068
(505) 869-4637

La Viña Winery
4201 S. Highway 28
La Union, NM 88021
575-882-7632
www.lavinawinery.com

Las Nutrias Winery
P.O. Box 1156
4627 Corrales Road
Corrales, NM 88048
505-897-7863
505-898-5690

Los Luceros Winery
P.O. Box 1100
Alcalde, NM 87511
505-852-1085
505-753-7925
Fax: 505-753-6863

Luna Rossa Winery
3710 W. Pine Street
Deming, NM 88030
575-544-1160
www.lunarossawinery.com

Mademoiselle Vineyards
    See Southwest Wines
www.mademoisellevineyards.com

Madison Vineyards & Winery
HRC 72 Box 490
Ribera, NM 87560
575-421-8028
http://madison-winery.com

Milagro Vineyards
985 West Ella
P.O. Box 1205
Corrales, NM 87048
Phone & Fax: 505-898-3998
www.milagrovineyardsandwinery.com

Ponderosa Valley Vineyards
& Winery
3171 Highway 290
Ponderosa, NM 87044
575-834-7487
Fax: 575-834-7073
1-800-WINE MKR
http://ponderosawinery.com

Sabinal Vineyards
25 Winery Road
Bosque, NM 87006
505-864-2816

San Ysidro Winery
223 Rio Bravo Dr.
Los Alamos, NM   87544
505-672-3678
Fax: 505-672-1482

Sandia Shadows Vineyard
& Winery
P.O. Box 92675
Albuquerque, NM 87199-2675
505-856-1006
Fax: 505-858-0859
Tasting Room:
11704 Coronado, NE
Albuquerque, NM 87122
(505) 298-8826

Santa Fe Vineyards
Route 1, Box 216A
Española, NM 87532
505-753-8100
800-477-2571
www.santafevineyards.com

Santa Rita Cellars
Wines of the Southwest
2641 Calle de Guadelupe
Mesilla, NM 88047
575-524-2408
877-NMWINES
www.santaritacellars.com

Sisneros-Torres Vineyards
P.O. Box 193
23 Winery Road North
Sabinal, NM 87006
505-861-3802
bert9436@msn.com

St. Clair Winery
    See Southwest Wines
www.stclairvineyards.com

Southwest Wines
New Mexico Wineries Inc.
P.O. Box 1180
Deming, NM 88031
575-546-9324
Fax: 575-546-7905
Wholesale Wines: 877-NMWINES
Wine Club: 888-SWWINES
www.southwestwines.com

Tularosa Vineyards
#23 Coyote Canyon Road
Tularosa, NM 88352
Phone: 575-585-2260
800-687-4467
www.tularosavineyards.com

Vivác Winery
2075 State Highway 68
Dixon, NM 87527
505-579-4441
Fax: 505-579-4575
www.vivacwinery.com

Vina Madre Winery
PO Box 2002
Roswell, NM 88202
(575) 622-7070

Willmon Vineyards
2801 Sudderth Drive
Ruidoso, NM 88345
Phone: 575-630-WINE

Wines of the San Juan
Tasting Room
233 Hwy 511
Blanco, NM 87412
505-632-0879
Fax: 505-632-8709
www.winesofthesanjuan.com

INDEX

ABOUT THE AUTHOR

Clyde W. Casey, who lives in Roswell, New Mexico, was born and raised in Colorado Springs, Colorado, of pioneer and Cherokee Indian heritage. Following attendance at Colorado College, he became a well-known author, professional entertainer, award-winning sculptor and energetic cook.

Art has been Casey's lifetime love and cooking—which he considers an art form—his special passion. His greatest sense of satisfaction and enjoyment comes from sharing his knowledge of New Mexico's colorful heritage and foods with others. He has published two other cookbooks, *New Mexico Cooking* and *Sassy Southwest Cooking*.

Involved in the art business for nearly 40 years, Casey was a sculptor of Western bronzes, an art gallery operator and a general promoter of the arts. A noted Western art historian and sculptural art restoration expert, he served for a number of years as president of the Professional Artists of Colorado. He also indulged his side interest—entertaining—by producing show segments for the Jaycee Chuckwagon in the Garden of the Gods Visitor and Nature Center by Pikes Peak. At one time he also picked guitar, sang, and wrote songs with a three-man group, the Trailriders.

Casey was involved in other ventures as well. He owned the first full-line pet store and grooming parlor in Colorado Springs. He also trapped rattlesnakes and shipped them live to a biological supply house for the production of anti-venom serum.

Always seeking new interests to challenge his inquisitive mind and intrigued by many visits to New Mexico, Casey made Roswell, New Mexico, his home about twenty years ago, helping to establish a bus manufacturing plant. He immediately began studying his new home state's history and culture. He retired in 2003 and now spends his time writing cookbooks and novels.

Clyde Casey lives with his wife, Millie, a prize-winning quilter, in Roswell. They have three grown children, five grandchildren and one great-grandchild. At home he works on perfecting his ever-growing collection of New Mexican recipes.